MASTERING THE IPHONE 12 PRO CAMERA

IPHONE PHOTOGRAPHY GUIDE TAKING PICTURES LIKE A PRO EVEN AS A SMARTPHONE BEGINNER

JAMES NINO

© 2020 James Nino

All rights reserved.

This book or any portion thereof may not be reproduced or used in any manner whatsoever without the express written permission of the publisher except for the use of brief quotations in a book review.

You are welcome to join the Fan's Corner, here

Mastering the iPhone 12 Pro Camera

iPhone Photography Guide Taking Pictures like a Pro Even as a SmartPhone Beginner

James Nino

Disclaimer

The advice and strategies found within may not be suitable for every situation. This work is sold with the understanding that neither the author nor the publisher is held responsible for the results accrued from the advice in this book.

All rights reserved. No part of this publication may be reproduced, distributed, or transmitted in any form or by any means, including photocopying, recording, or other electronic or mechanical methods, without the prior written permission of the publisher, except in the case of brief quotations embodied in critical reviews and certain other noncommercial uses permitted by copyright law.

Introduction

Hey, congratulation on purchasing Mastering the iPhone 12 Pro Camera book. This book is a must-have book for anyone who wants to use his or her iPhone 12 Pro to start taking stunning photos.

This book will open your eyes to many of the basic functions that the iPhone 12 Pro camera can be used for as well as some advanced functions that may not be too obvious to users of the iPhone 12 Pro. For those who already have older versions of the iPhone and have difficulty locating some of their favorite icons, this book will show you where they have been moved to and the most effective ways of using them to take amazing pictures.

Quite often, the manuals shipped with our devices tend not to do enough justice to the subject of the device at other times, they can be overwhelming. Many other "Get Started Guides" are sometimes too thin and do not really solve any problem, which is why this book is a real gem.

This book will get you acquainted with the mobile phone you carry around you that you can also use for your photography device whenever you go on a trip, attend an event, visit a location, or casting a scene. Knowing how to get more from the digital camera in your pocket is what this book is about, after all, after spending so much to get your iPhone 12 Pro, you naturally would want to get more out of it.

This book will help you know how to use the camera on your iPhone 12 Pro better and help you optimize the camera features in a lot more ways than you have ever imagined.

As you open the pages of this book, you will be exposed to a wide range of fantastic photos and video tools that you had probably overlooked as ordinary symbols to a position where you now know how to use them.

For those who order this book while on vacation, this book can help you improve on your use of your iPhone camera, especially for those things you did not know it could do. You will find that this book is quite worth the time and money spent on it and highly recommended to anyone who uses their iPhone 12 Pro to take pictures. You can start using your iPhone 12 Pro camera and start taking the kind of photos that nobody will even believe were shot by you with an iPhone.

Contents to Expect

Chapter 1 1

   Introducing the iPhone 12 Pro 1

   Design of the iPhone 12 Pro Camera 6

   iPhone 12 Pro Cameras 6

   Versatility of the Camera System 8

   Realistic AR and Innovative Camera Experiences 9

   iPhone 12 Pro Tech Specs 10

   The iPhone 12 Pro's Technical Specs 10

   The iPhone 12's Pro Design and Display 12

   iPhone 12 Pro Camera 13

   iPhone 12 PRO HDR Feature 15

   Utilizing the HDR Mode On iPhone 12 Pro 16

Chapter 2 18

   About the Apple iPhone 12 Pro Camera 18

   Apple iPhone 12 Pro Camera Features 21

   Relevant Camera Settings to Know 22

   DSLR VS iPhone 12 Pro 28

   Who is the iPhone 12 Pro Suited for 29

Chapter 3 30

   Capturing Photos on iPhone 12 Pro 30

iPhone 12 Pro Camera Modes 30
Switching Between the Lenses 37
Switching to the Standard Wide-Angle Lens 38
Switching to the Ultra-Wide-Angle Lens 38
Switching to the Telephoto Lens 39
Fine Tuning the zoom in and Out 40
Expanding your Photoshoot Scene 43
Introducing the LIDAR Sensor 43
Scanning QR Codes with your iPhone 57
Expanding the Capability of the Front Camera 58
Mirroring Front Camera 59

Chapter 4 60
Manipulating Images on iPhone 12 Pro 60
Editing a Photo or Video 61
Before and After Effects of Photo Edits 61
Take Screenshots 62
Knowing the Different Cropping Options 63
Straightening and Adjusting Perspective 64
How to Use Filters Correctly 64
Reverting to an Original Photo or Video 71
Changing the Aspect Ratio 72
Indicator for Camera Rolling 72

Chapter 5 74

Additional Controls on the Camera App 74

Learn to Take Great Selfies All by Yourself 74

Selfie Cameras 77

Taking a Slofie 78

Switching Between Close and Wide-Angle Selfies 79

Utilizing the Night Mode 80

Live Photos and Having Fun with Them 83

Taking a Live Photo 84

Editing a Live Photo 84

To Edit Live Photos 85

Viewing a Live Photo 86

Viewing Custom Effects of a Live Photo 86

Types of Live Photo Effects 87

Taking a Panorama Photo 88

Slow Motion Video 88

Recording a Slow-motion Video 90

Understanding iPhone 12 Pro Camera Focus 91

Adjusting the Camera Focus 91

Manually Adjusting the Camera Focus 92

Understanding iPhone 12 Camera Exposure 94

How to Adjust the Camera Exposure 96

How to Lock Camera Focus and Exposure Separately 97
How to Use the Self-Timer 98
Having Fun with Your iPhone 12 Pro 99
How to Create your Own Memoji 100
To Edit, Duplicate, or Delete a Memoji 103
Sending Animated Animoji or Memoji Recordings 104

Chapter 6 108
Configuring Other Camera Settings 108
Accessing Hidden Camera Controls 109
Using the HDR Feature 112
The Portrait Mode on iPhone 12 Pro 115
Blurring Photos Backgrounds with Portrait Mode 116
Adjusting Portrait Photos 117
How Not to Include the Blur 119
Low-Light Photos with Night Mode On iPhone 12 Pro 121

Chapter 7 123
Getting the Most of Your iPhone 12 Pro 123
Best Practices for Smartphone Photography 124

Chapter 7 132
iPhone 12 Videography 132
Video Quality 133
How to Shoot Videos with your iPhone 12 Pro 133

Professional iPhone 12 Pro Videos 137
Image Stabilization 138
Dolby Vision 139
Drone Photography with the iPhone 12 Pro 140
Wedding Photographs with the iPhone 12 Pro 141
Chapter 8 146
Third-party Camera Apps 146
Caring for Your iPhone Camera 148
Conclusion 151

Chapter 1

Introducing the iPhone 12 Pro

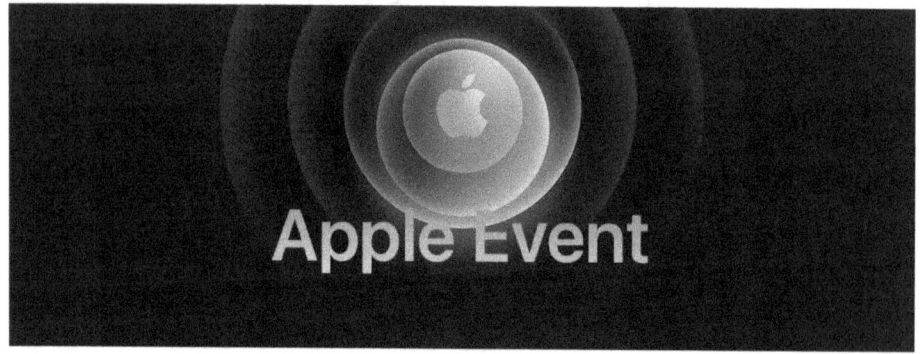

Apple in October of 2020 announced its iPhone 12s' line up, ranging from iPhone 12, iPhone 12 Pro, and iPhone 12 Pro Max. All these smartphones are the best phones you are going to find in the market.

Apple is known for its quality products and they have not disappointed their fans this time too. Everything in the smartphone is at its best. Though Apple had to face critics for not giving a charging adapter along with the smartphones, Apple still managed to satisfy their fans with the awesome design and quality.

The build of the iPhone 12 series reminds us of the iPhone 5s. The sharp cut edges that seem to have been abandoned in subsequent releases after the iPhone 5s was reintroduced in this iPhone and has been the talking point of the phone since then and appreciated by millions of iPhone fans all over the world. It is hard to get your eyes off the attractive form of the phone and the camera set up that characterizes all three phones.

Apple announced everything regarding the cameras in the official event held in October. Guess what; this time, iPhone cameras have added more features than ever experienced in an iPhone.

The stunning features and quality capture have even impressed professional photographers. If you are already from an iPhone family, then you might be aware of the quality of pictures. This time in iPhone 12 series, the inclusion of telephoto lenses has made fans crazy for it.

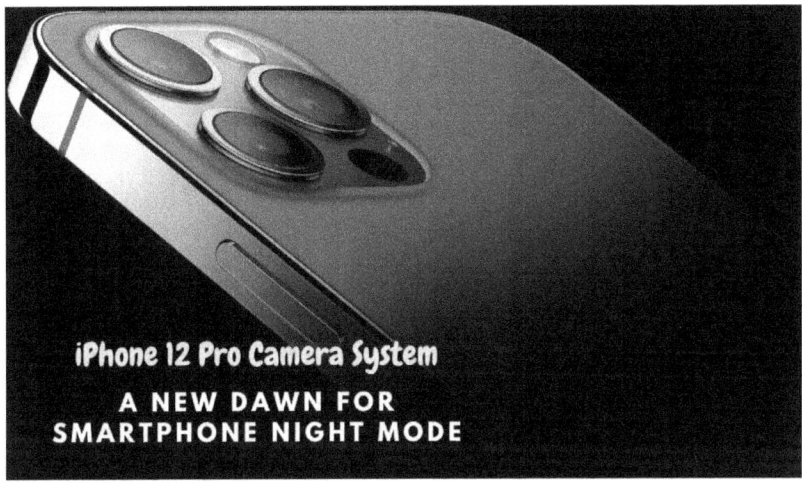

Figure 1: iPhone 12 Pro Lenses

Even though the whole lineup of the iPhone 12 series has got the best of the cameras in their respective segments, however, the iPhone 12 Pro has got such remarkable features that serious lovers of photography admire. Being a photography enthusiast, I tend to prefer the iPhone 12 Pro camera among the three, mostly because of its size and shape.

The camera setup is incredibly better than previous iPhones and best suits the design of the smartphone body. Be it tapping the low light photos or zooming the street captures; everything is up to mark.

Who doesn't love night portraits? The iPhone 12 pro camera is able to take some of the best night portraits ever taken by a phone camera with its portrait mode. The telephoto lens helps you capture scenes with very little detail. Apple is known for its quality products and they have continued their tradition of quality in this iPhone 12 Pro.

Well, you all might be thinking that why am I highlighting iPhone 12 Pro cameras again and again. Guys, the iPhone 12 Pro's camera have got exceptional features. You can record more spectacular videos using iPhone 12 Pro, as it comes equipped with a Dolby vision recording that has 60 times more colors. I would be telling you in detail everything that makes iPhone 12 pro's camera the best in the market right now. If you want to make the best of your iPhone 12 pro cameras, then stick with me to the end of this book.

Using the iPhone 12 Pro to take pictures is as easy as it's always been in previous versions of the iPhones only that now you can make it do more than those versions if you only knew how to find your way around the interface. Compared to what you may be used to in earlier versions of the iPhone, some controls and settings in the iPhone 12 Pro no longer exist while many others have been moved to new locations, including some changes in the layout of the phone's camera app. The camera app on the iPhone 12 Pro is at first glance similar to the old iPhone Camera app only that the new app has a great deal of depth, which makes it able to take crisp photos with minimal effort even when the lighting is limited.

Software and interface changes are not the only things that differentiate the iPhone 12 Pro from other iPhone versions. The cameras on the iPhone were already very good at taking great daytime pictures, but the new iPhone 12 Pro takes their photography to a whole new level. This is mostly because of the triple-lens setup at the back of the iPhone 12 Pro and the supersonic A14 Bionic that enables the phone to expand its capabilities.

To take advantage of these hardware features is an expanded new iOS 14 operating system that enables it to produce crystal clear pictures, among other new functions like the Night mode on all lenses and the Quick Take video. There is also a unique feature that allows users to zoom out on an image even though you had previously captured it with some parts that seem to be missing.

These hardware and software make the iPhone 12 Pro to be touted to be one of the best iPhones ever to be produced by Apple when you consider the ingenuity in combining technology with the phone's high-level photography. The majority of the iPhone's 12 Pro functions involve knowing what and how to tap, which is what helps to ensure that the photos shot with the iPhone 12 Pro even if taken by a novice come out crisp, amazing and sharp. This phone runs on iOS 14 with a high-level dual-sensor for the rear cameras and is also powered by Apple's new A14 Bionic chip.

The four available colors for the iPhone 12 Pro for buyers to choose from include blue, gold, graphite, and silver.

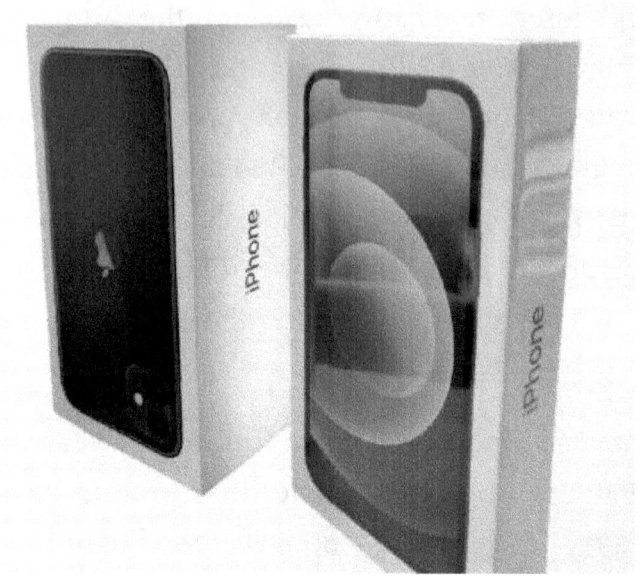

Figure 2: Unboxing the iPhone 12 Pro

According to Apple, the iPhone 12 Pro is made from the toughest glass ever to grace the glass body of a smartphone and offers an amazing resistance to dust and water with its IP rating of IP68, which helps to improve its reliability and durability.

It's rated to be able to stay up to a depth of water of up to 2M or 6.5 feet for a period of up to 30 minutes. Although an IP68 rating can withstand immersion in water, it is advisable to limit the phone's exposure to water to just splashes, accidental exposure to liquid, and maybe rain.

For sounds, it equally supports Dolby Atmos and Spatial audio, which enables it to offer a truly impressive sound experience.

Design of the iPhone 12 Pro Camera

The iPhone 12 series is totally for photos and videos. The sharp design of the device and those three camera lenses along with the LIDAR sensor will surely win your heart. The camera lenses are installed on the top-left corner of the rear side as they were in iPhone 11 pro max.

iPhone 12 Pro Cameras

There are 3 cameras on the iPhone 12 pro, including a flashlight and LIDAR Scanner. These cameras include an Ultra-wide camera, a telephoto camera, and a wide camera. These cameras have a 6x zoom and focus lens to make the shots better. Let us have a look at their features and their functions.

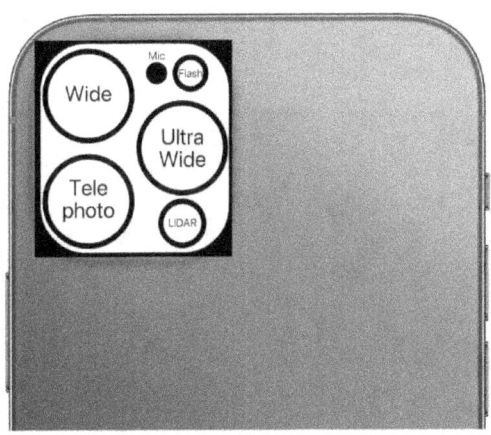

Figure 3: iPhone 12 Pro Layout

Ultra-Wide Camera

The ultra-wide camera has a 120-degree field of view that helps you in capturing extra-wide-angle shots.

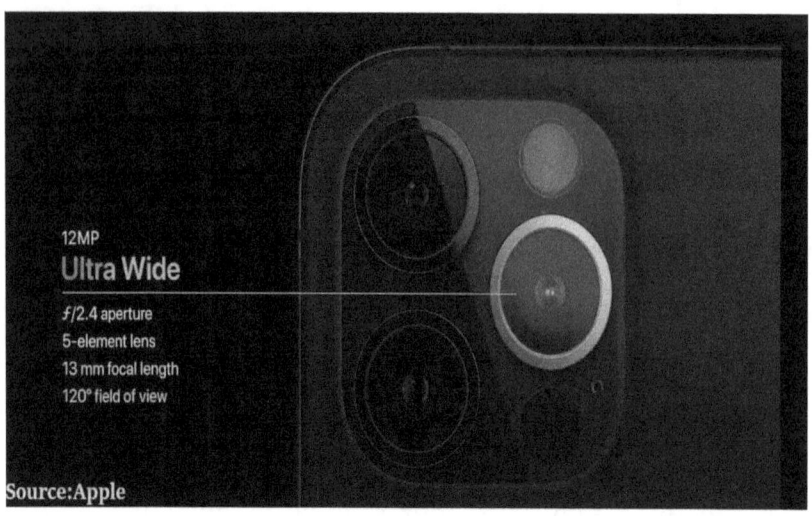

Figure 4: Identifying the 12MP Ultra-wide Lens

Wide Camera

The wide camera has a 7-element lens with optical image stabilization and 100 focus pixels.

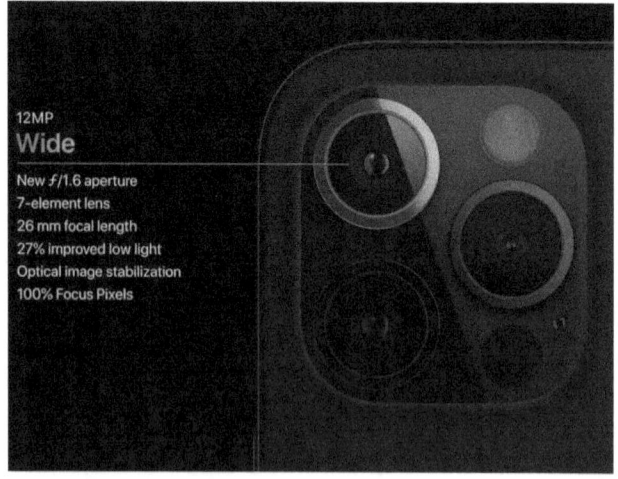

Figure 5: Identifying the 12MP Wide Lens

Telephoto Camera

The telephoto camera is for taking stunning portraits and square pictures. It consists of a 6-element lens.

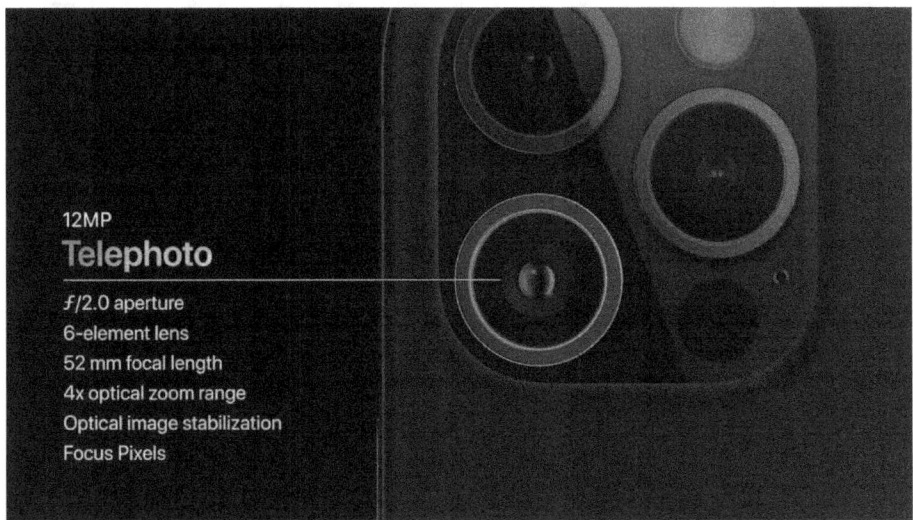

Figure 6: Identifying the 12MP Telephoto Lens

The neat and clean design of the iPhone 12 Pro makes it look elegant. The cameras are placed in the same position as the iPhone 11 Pro Max, but when compared with the iPhone 11 Pro Max; iPhone 12 Pro has a bigger image sensor, a faster main camera lens, and better image stabilization. Autofocus also has an improvement with the LIDAR sensor.

Versatility of the Camera System

The camera hardware is powered by the super A14 Bionic with a new image signal processor, which helps in improving image quality and other popular photography features that are not possible with general cameras. It also includes the Apple Pro Raw, which allows users to exercise better control over colors, details, and dynamic range on the iPhone or other photo editing apps.

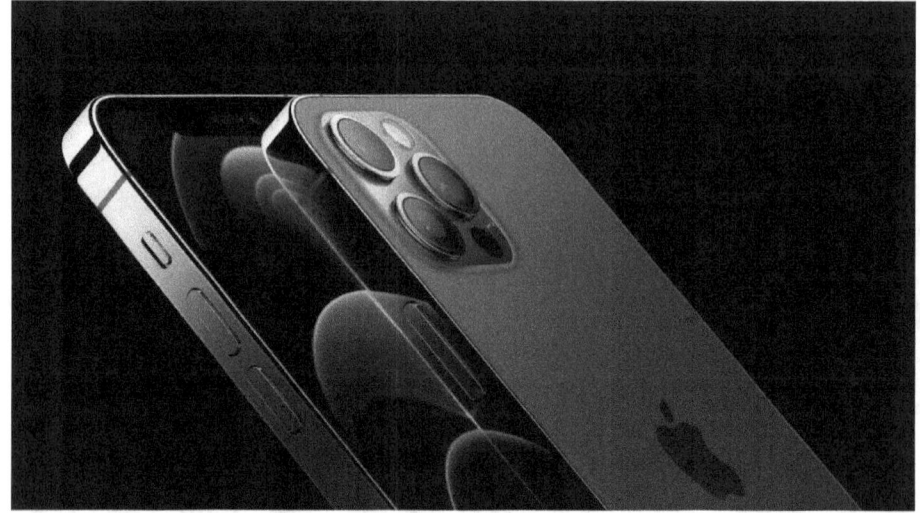

Figure 7: iPhone 12 Rear Cameras

The iPhone 12 Pro also offers the best quality video shooting through its end-to-end HDR video with Dolby vision up to 60 FPS and comes with better stabilization. Well, more about this will be discussed when we dive more into the video capabilities of the iPhone in the videos section.

Realistic AR and Innovative Camera Experiences

The new LIDAR scanner measures light distance and makes use of pixel depth information of a view. This helps in faster and more realistic, as well as reliable AR experiences, and also improves autofocus by 6x in low lights for more accuracy and reducing the capture time of the photos. This amazing LIDAR scanner unlocks various night mode portraits, which help in rendering a low light Bokeh effect.

iPhone 12 Pro Tech Specs

Apple has brought a lot of new exciting features and hardware changes in its most recent lineup. If you are someone who is switching from Android to iPhone 12 Pro or an existing iPhone user and finding it hard to get used to these newly introduced changes in tech specs and design of iPhone 12 Pro, let me walk you through all the new changes - technical aspects and specifications.

The iPhone 12 Pro's Technical Specs

The iPhone 12 Pro is a 6.1-inch touchscreen Apple phone that comes shipped with the iOS 14 and is powered by a hex-core Apple A14 Bionic CPU. As at the time of writing this book, this processor is acclaimed to be Apple's fastest chip in the market which allows it to give the iPhone 12 its superior performance and support for the graphical demands of the iPhone 12 Pro.

The iPhone 12 Pro features dual GSM SIMs for Nano-SIM and eSIM cards.

The iPhone 12 Pro is a pioneer in its supports for the 5G technology, which is the fastest technology compared to the iPhone 11 Pro's support for the 4G LTE network. This is one of the main features with which no other phone can be compared with the iPhone 12 series.

The Intel modem chip that comes with iPhone 12 Pro supports Gigabit-class LTE, 802.12 a/b/g/n/ac Wi-Fi 6 support, Band 40 support, Bluetooth 5.0, and UI ultra-wideband chip for better spatial awareness with better indoor tracking capabilities. It also has sensors that it uses for its gyroscope, ambient light sensor, accelerometer, compass/ magnetometer, barometer, and proximity sensor. Not to be left out is its support for face unlocks with 3D face recognition.

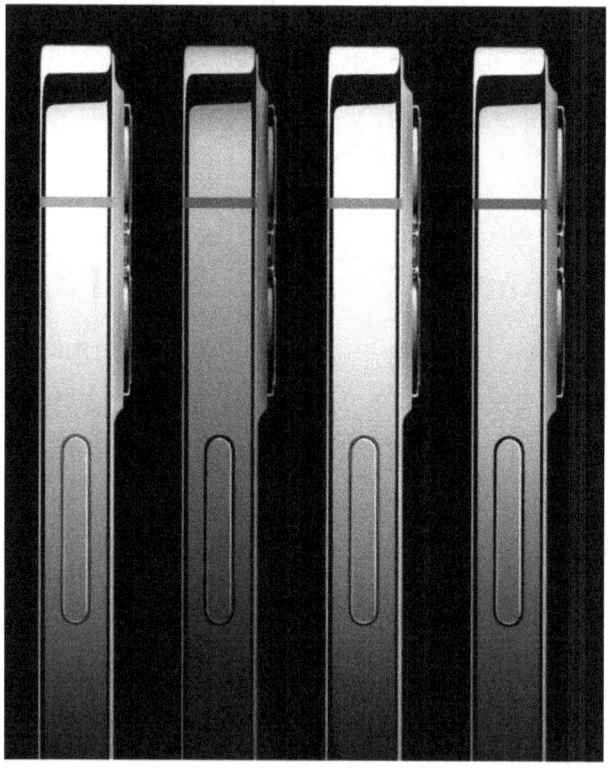

Figure 8: Various Colors for Shipping iPhone 12

The iPhone 12 Pro has support for Qi wireless charging, including proprietary MagSafe fast charging.

The battery life of the iPhone 12 Pro is terrific and is powered by a non-removable 2815mAh battery.

The iPhone 12's Pro Design and Display

The iPhone 12 Pro shares similar physical attributes as its predecessor iPhone 5s but has a noticeable camera bump on its back that houses the triple camera array, which is not present on the iPhone 5s but was introduced in the iPhone 11 series.

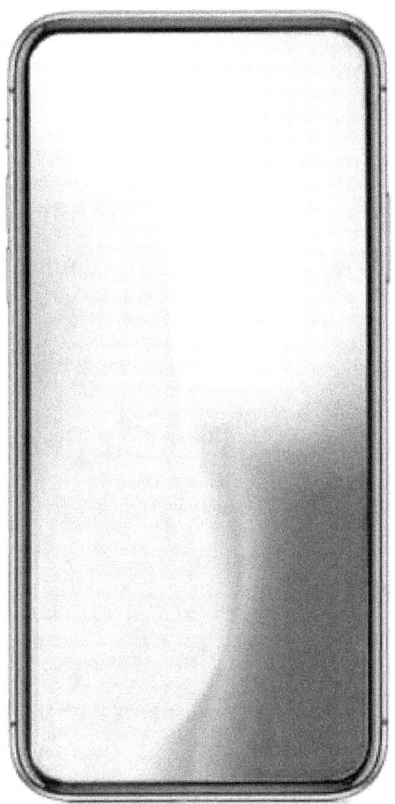

Figure 9: iPhone Screen Display with Resolution

Such camera bumps are not entirely new in the mobile phone industry, as a matter of fact, was introduced in the earlier version of iPhone 11 in response to the demands of many iPhone enthusiasts who wanted Apple to improve the quality of the iPhone's camera, especially when compared to other Android phones. However, unlike the camera bump of Samsung Galaxy S10, Huawei P30 Pro, and other Chinese manufacturing competitors, that of the iPhone 12 Pro is considerably chunkier.

The phone comes with a resolution of 2532 x 1170 pixels and a pixel density of 440 pixels per inch (PPI) with a contrast ratio of 1M:1 for its LCD. Similar to the iPhone 11 series, Apple continued the "Super Retina XDR" on its iPhone 12 Pro OLED Multi-Touch display. The display equally has support for Apple's newest advancement in technology that allows for tapping to wake up or activate the screen, Haptic Touch, swipe gesture in place of the Touch ID Home button, a wide color range that enables it to provide a realistic color and a True Tone, useful in matching the ambient light to the display's white balance.

iPhone 12 Pro Camera

If there is one feature that was consistently highlighted as a significant advantage over previous editions of the iPhone, it has to be the iPhone 12 Pro's camera or cameras. The iPhone 12 Pro comes with three rear cameras that include the standard wide-angle camera, an ultra-wide-angle camera with a 120-degree field of view, and a telephoto camera lens. Switching between these cameras is, however, remarkably easy and can be executed by flips of on-screen buttons.

The ultra-wide-angle camera can capture up to six times more scenes compared to what the standard wide-angle lens can capture from the same distance from the subject, which makes it a good way of capturing architecture images, landscape photos, tight shots, group pictures, and many other creative pictures.

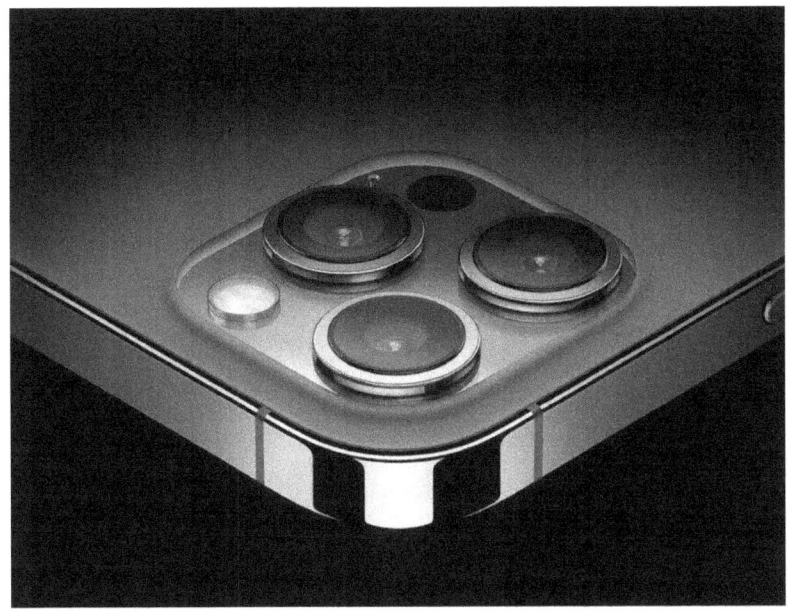

Figure 10: Triple iPhone Camera Array

The iPhone 12 Pro's camera interface has also undergone some changes that allow users to have that great user experience when trying to capture scenes outside the frame through the use of the ultra-wide-angle camera. The iPhone 12 Pro has a 6x optical zoom in and zooms out the range, and its range of the digital zoom is about 10x. It also contains a LiDAR scanner to provide a better night mode experience.

The portrait mode helps you capture photos with a clear focus on the subject and blurred background with bokeh and depth-control.

The addition by Apple of a new Night Mode that takes advantage of the iPhone's high processing capabilities combined with the new wide camera sensor to create crisp, bright, clear photos even in conditions that have very low lighting.

The iPhone 12 Pro also comes with Smart HDR 3, which allows for better recognition of people by differentiating them from the rest of the shot. Even though this feature preserves the background elements, it tends to ensure that faces retain their natural-looking skin tones, highlights, shadows, and gestures. The Smart HDR 3 uses machine learning in the capturing of natural-looking images that help improve the highlight and shadow detail.

iPhone 12 PRO HDR Feature

The iPhone 12 Pro was one of the most awaited smartphones of 2020, quite frankly, all variants of the iPhone are flagships when compared with their competitors. The iPhone 12 Pro comes with features and specifications that include, but not limited to; super retina XDR OLED, HDR10, 800 nits (typical), 1200 nits (peak) display, 6GB RAM, and the A14 Bionic chip. DxO mark rating for iPhone 12 pro is 128, putting it in one of the top five phones featured till now.

(It has been tested in every condition possible, DXO mark ratings are reliable because of how much work they put into trying out the different features in a phone. They even take pictures at a different time of day to effectively test a phone.)

As already explained; HDR stands for "High dynamic range" and is a way of how an image is further processed.

While HDR is on, every photo you take on your iPhone will be optimized automatically and will be balanced with a better exposure setup. This iPhone 12 Pro can take advantage of Dolby Vision HDR recording.

Starting with Dolby's vision, it is the first mobile to feature Dolby HDR video recording. It can shoot and edit as well.

On iPhone 12 Pro, you can record Dolby Vision 4K at 60 fps, but iPhone 12 is limited to 30 fps. We talked a lot about HDR, So, what is HDR? The answer is as simple as it gets.

A common scenario would be if you want to take a photo of someone in front of a beautiful scene and when doing so may mean that they'll be exposed to overly bright backlighting. Rather than choosing between where to focus; the background or image, or vice-versa. HDR makes it possible so you can get both in one photoshoot.

Utilizing the HDR Mode On iPhone 12 Pro

HDR mode consecutively takes pictures at different exposures such as normal light that allows adjustment for the darkest and brightest details, then taking advantage of its A14 Bionic chip that is able to apply advanced computational mathematics to mix the different shots and produce a stunning photographic effect.

For a person who shoots outdoors, the iPhone 12 Pro provides a technology that is called "Smart HDR 3". Older HDR software was dreadful, at least when compared with the Smart HDR3, which made images look manipulated.

Technically Defining HDR

HDR 3 uses machine learning (ML) technology of the real-world to train its neural engine, a component on its microprocessor A14

Bionic. When you use your iPhone to consistently take pictures of a particular type of scene, after a while it starts to recognize specific scenes and then automatically create the right exposure for each one. So, when you go on your travels, those of mountains, clouds, snow become recognized easily with the help of HDR3.

Putting it in another way, you can shoot something which you have shot before, and it will know by itself what exposure would be better without the need for toning.

There is something called 'Deep Fusion' also, which means instead of just combining images and providing final output. It selects the best pixels for the colors, sharpness, highlights, and shadows before telling the engine to combine those pixels into the final photograph.

Chapter 2

About the Apple iPhone 12 Pro Camera

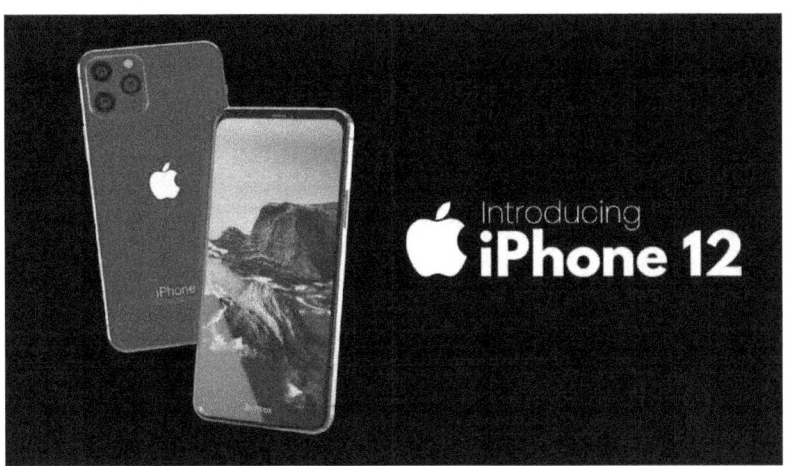

The iPhone 12 Pro has one front camera and three rear cameras. The front camera uses a TrueDepth Camera System, which aids its Face ID recognition feature in the improvement of the phone's security. Face ID is now a lot faster than previous versions and works from a much farther distance, wider angle range, and still very secure. That means that the phone is now able to recognize you even from a considerable distance from the phone and can open itself when you are walking towards it.

The front-facing 12-megapixel camera of the iPhone 12 Pro is an upgrade to the 7-megapixel camera that came with the iPhone XR, which makes it suitable to be used for both selfies and slofies.

The iPhone 12 Pro camera has one of the best cameras ever found in any smartphone. The triple camera set up along with the LIDAR scanner can shoot excellent images with zero noise.

There are different modes to shoot according to your environment. You just need to configure the right settings on your device, and you are good to go. Camera Settings of the default camera app on the iPhone12 pro are not so difficult to configure.

The iPhone 12 Pro's new front-facing camera makes it easy to switch from portrait mode into landscape mode and vice versa, which allows for the capturing of more objects within a frame. It is equally able to capture 120 fps slo-mo videos, which is what enables a new feature call Slofies.

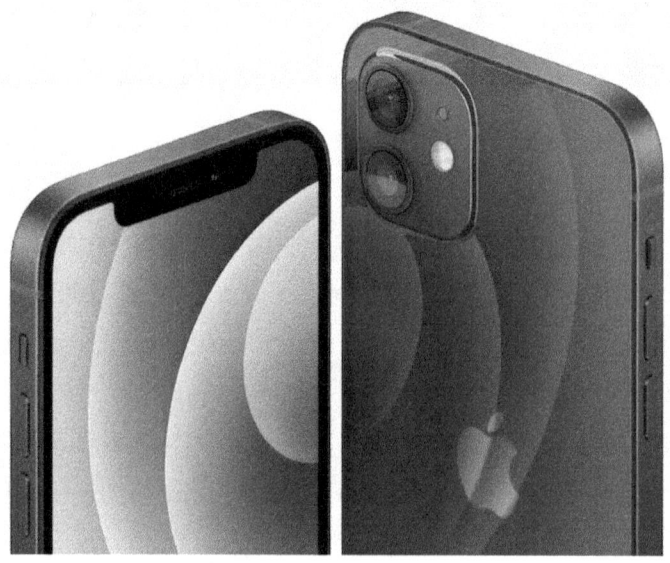

Figure 11: iPhone 12 Pro with Amazing Capability

These slow-motion videos are similar to the slo-mo videos associated with the rear-facing camera in previous iPhones. The new camera is, however, capable of recording up to 60 fps videos when in 4k mode and provides support for extended dynamic range videos at 30 fps.

Slofie is not the only feature the iPhone 12 Pro's TrueDepth Camera System supports, it also has support for animated 3D emoji characters called Animoji and Memoji, which are frequently used to simulate the way we want a person's face to appear. Where Animoji provides animal styled emojis, Memoji offers customizable avatars that the user can personalize.

The iPhone 12 Pro model is the first Apple phone to have an upgraded triple-lens rear camera system that includes a primary camera with an f/1.8 6-element 12-megapixel wide-angle lens with a focal length of 26mm which is equivalent to a 13mm DSLR lens, a second camera with an f/2.4 5-element 12-megapixel ultra-wide-angle lens and a focal length of 13mm and a third camera with an f/2.0 aperture 12-megapixel teleport lens. The telephoto lens has support for 2x optical zoom out even though it does not have the optical zoom feature. The iPhone 12 Pro also has support for a front-facing f/2.2 aperture 12-megapixel camera for selfies and pictures from the front.

The iPhone 12 Pro model also uses its standard wide-angle camera to support Optical Image Stabilization. The combination of the standard wide-angle lens, teleport photos, and the ultra-wide-angle lens is what gives the iPhone 12 Pro its powerful camera capabilities.

The triple-lens system on the iPhone 12 Pro models makes it more suitable for capturing portrait images of many people by using its Wide and Telephoto framing in Portrait Mode.

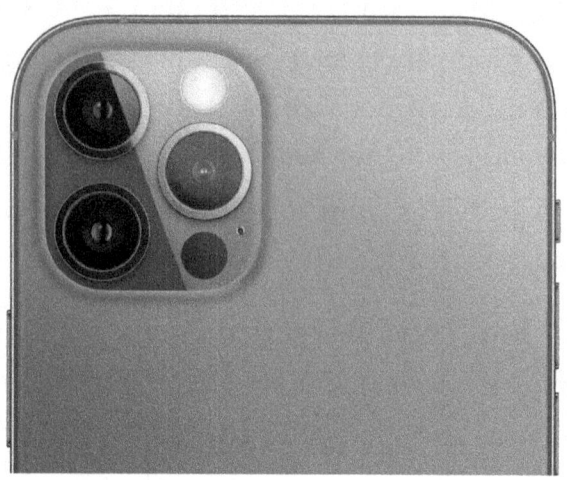

Figure 12: The Three Camera Types of iPhone 12 Pro

Apple iPhone 12 Pro Camera Features

One outstanding feature of the iPhone 12 camera is its ability to capture a space that is up to four times more than a standard camera view can capture by using its ultra-wide feature.

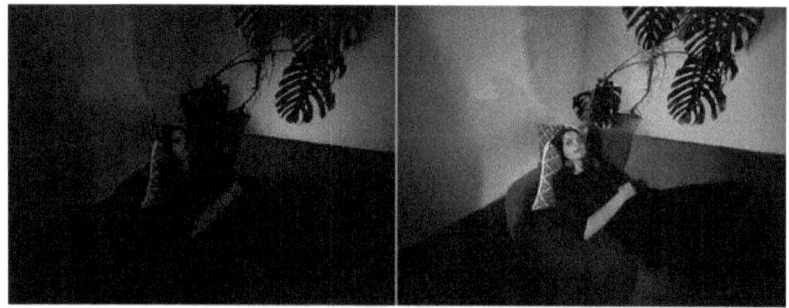

Figure 13: Comparing Night Mode On and Night Mode Off

Another outstanding feature the iPhone 12 Pro has over its predecessors is its ability to capture pictures even in the dark, using intelligent machine learning, the computational algorithm that makes the phone take multiple shots in night mode and then fuse them to create a crisp, clear and visible image from objects that even the naked eye cannot see because of how dark the environment is. So, when next you are in a dark room, and you suspect there is someone or something else there, you can just take a shot in the direction you suspect the object is located and take a picture.

Nonetheless, photos are not the only area where the iPhone 12 Pro excels, there is equally a new QuickTake feature that enables users to take rapid video clips without having to switch to video mode when taking still pictures by tapping and holding the shutter button quickly.

Lovers of social media will love the slow-motion selfie videos which Apple has decided to call slofies. This feature uses the TrueDepth camera capability of the 12-megapixel sensor front camera, which also has support for 4k video capture.

Relevant Camera Settings to Know

The iPhone 12 Pro has a very powerful camera that requires a user knowing how to effectively take advantage of it by learning how to tweak the iPhone camera settings. Many of these settings are not peculiar to the iPhone cameras alone, they are also useful in the photography world and among photo enthusiasts.

Focus

This is a very dominant feature in any camera for someone that wants to take pictures that are crystal clear, not less when the person is using an iPhone 12 Pro.

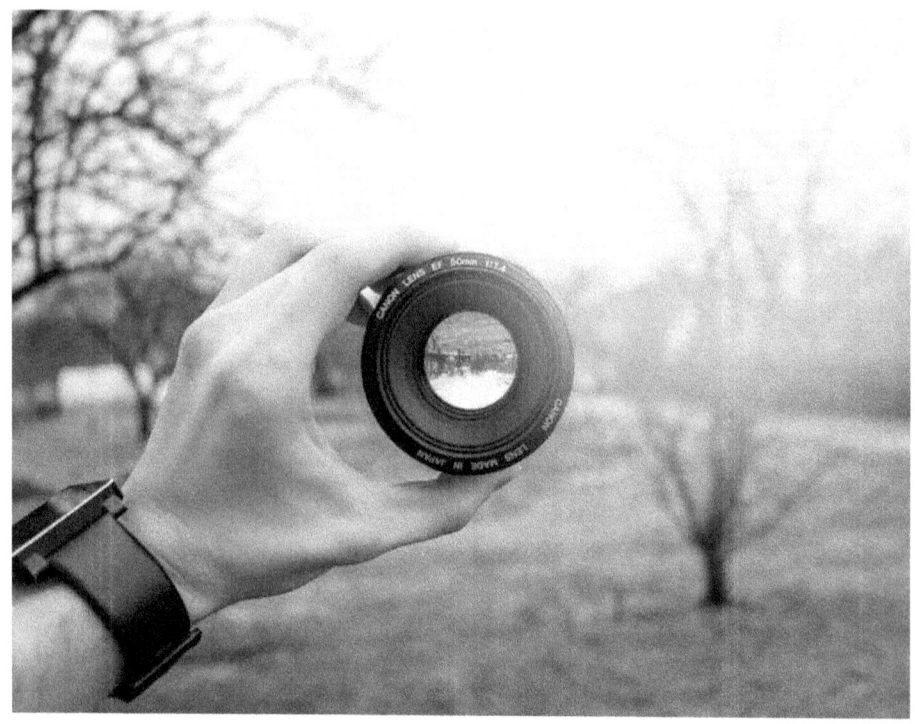

Figure 14: Camera Focus for Digital Camera

Failure to consider focus can lead to blurry images that can affect the reputation of the iPhone camera.

Those who are not camera professionals are, however, able to get by because of the tremendous depth of field that the iPhone 12 Pro has, which makes it able to ensure that both the background and the foreground are sharp with its automatic feature.

Exposure

Another critical feature that photographers play around with when utilizing cameras is exposure. Although many digital cameras can adjust their camera's exposure automatically, many other users prefer to be able to control that themselves, especially when the camera is not able to get it on its own.

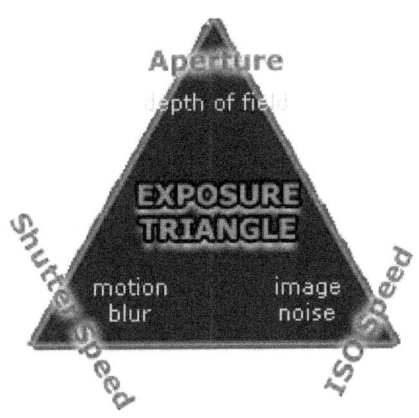

Figure 15: Exploring the Exposure Feature of Cameras

The Exposure Slider for the iPhone 12 Pro makes it possible for users to manually control the camera's exposure, thereby overriding the iPhone's exposure settings.

The exposure slider is generally handy when correcting the brightness of a shot even though you can equally use it to over or underexpose a shot when trying to achieve a specific visual effect.

Filters

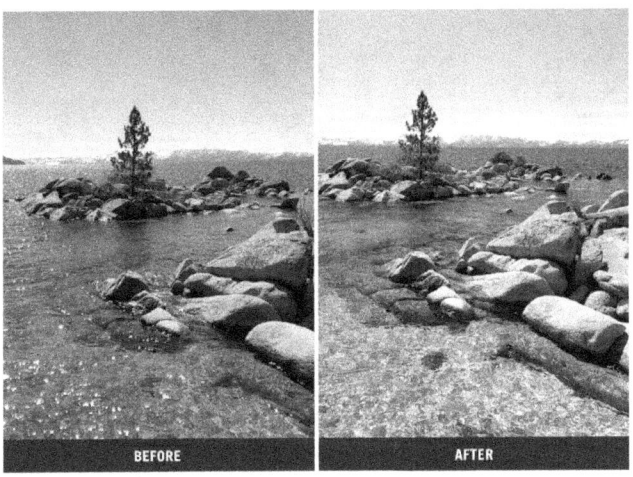

Figure 16: Enhance Photos Using Filter Option

This means the preset filters on the app can be applied even at the point of taking pictures or Live Mode.

Self-Timer

The iPhone 12 Pro comes with the filter option even though inferior to the filters offered by programs like Instagram, it can apply filters in changing the hues in your pictures using the Camera app on the iPhone.

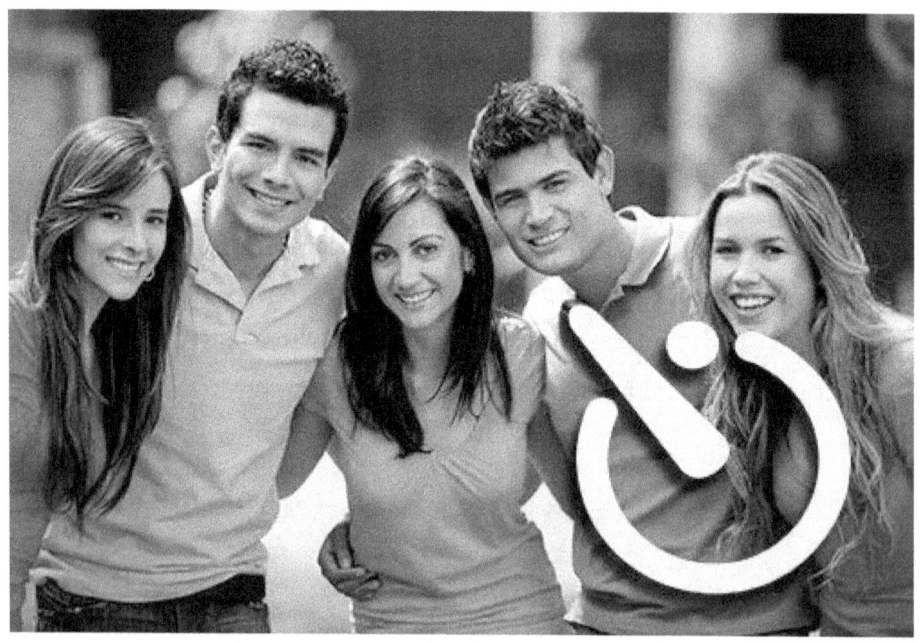

Figure 17: Take Pictures using Self Timer

It is time to take a family picture, only that there is no stranger around to help capture the shot. This is an example of many other situations where the self-timer can be used.

The self-timer feature is one of the options you find at the top right corner of the camera app on the iPhone 12's Pro screen.

High Dynamic Range (HDR)

The HDR is beneficial for capturing shots in very tricky lighting conditions where manual adjustments and automatic settings are unable to control the exposure levels. You will find the HDR useful in high-contrast lightings like sunsets, sunrise, and overcast scenes.

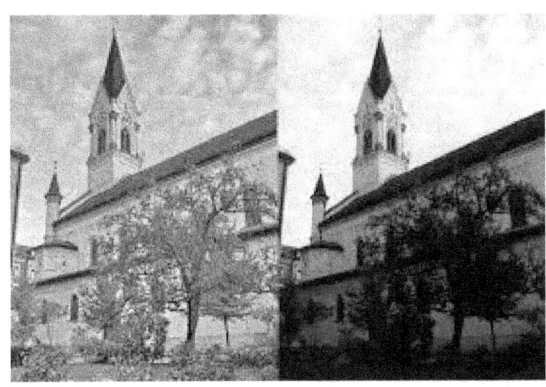

Figure 18: HDR Feature of the iPhone 12 Pro

By activating the HDR, it prompts the phone to capture three different photos with varying exposure levels, which are then composed together to create a clear image with the right exposure.

Rule of Thirds

One of the fundamentals of photography is composition, which in short means; the placement of different objects in a frame which makes it look aesthetically pleasing.

The idea is to take the photos in such a way that the subject is placed in such a place in the frame, which looks good to the human eye. To understand this, photographers often use the rule of thirds and the golden ratio. These are not limited to photography, it is an important part of creating any kind of visual art.

To help you compose your photos better, all cameras, and smartphones have grid lines on the screen. You can turn on the gridlines from the camera settings. There are three horizontal and three vertical lines on the screen. To apply the rule of thirds, your objective is to ensure that the subject that you want to photograph falls on any of the intersections of the lines. This produces a much more natural image, which is subtle and aesthetic.

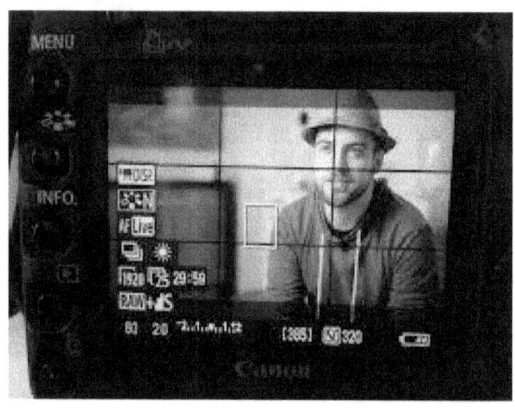

Figure 19: Taking Advantage of Gridlines in Taking Shots

When using grid lines, you only need to position the main subject on any of the lines in the grid intersections.

The Golden Ratio

The golden ratio is a much harder topic to grasp, but the general idea is similar to the rule of thirds, only in this case, you don't divide the frame into 1:1:1, but you divide it into 1:0.6:1. This method is most useful for landscape photography, nature photography, and a few other situations where you have a larger area to cover.

DSLR VS iPhone 12 Pro

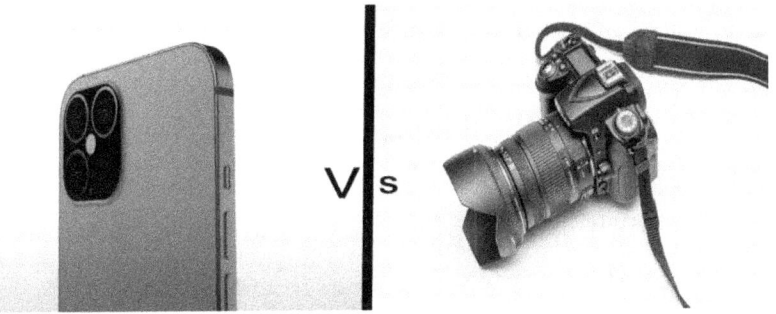

Figure 20: iPhone Camera vs DSLR

DSLR cameras have been the industry standard for a long time, it was unimaginable that any smartphone camera could compete with it. People that were hitherto interested in photography had to buy very expensive cameras, and then they had to buy expensive and heavy lenses to go with it. It was also a pain to carry it with you, it barely even could fit in the bag. However, with the invention of such high-quality smartphone cameras, all the power of the DSLR camera now comes in the palm of your hands.

Popular Youtuber, Peter McKinnon, who is a professional photographer, recently created a video where he reviewed the iPhone 12 Pro, and in that video, he was able to confirm that the iPhone could be just as good as his professional camera.

Another YouTuber, Justine also reviewed the camera and has directly compared it to a DSLR camera. The flexibility of the lens, the reliable video quality, and the amazing autofocus all combine to make the iPhone 12 Pro smartphone camera, one of the best on offer, not only among the smartphones but also among cameras in general.

Who is the iPhone 12 Pro Suited for

The iPhone 12 pro has one of the most reliable smartphone cameras ever. Starting from the excellent hardware to the smooth software. Everything about the iPhone camera is amazing, to say the least. As mentioned before, some photographers are taking wedding photos with the iPhone these days, and not to mention that the iPhone is used by many vloggers and YouTubers.

With the rise of TikTok, the iPhone has become a rage among youngsters who love to make TikTok videos. Honestly, the iPhone 12 Pro camera is good enough to be the only camera you ever need. It is unbelievably useful in so many different situations and so many scenarios. Even travel bloggers will find it very useful as part of their travel gear and be able to use just their iPhones to film entire videos and also take all their Instagram photos.

The iPhone 12 Pro is a phone for everyone, whether you are just interested in a phone with a camera, or you want a professional quality camera, or you are an aspiring videographer, it is suitable for everyone.

Chapter 3

Capturing Photos on iPhone 12 Pro

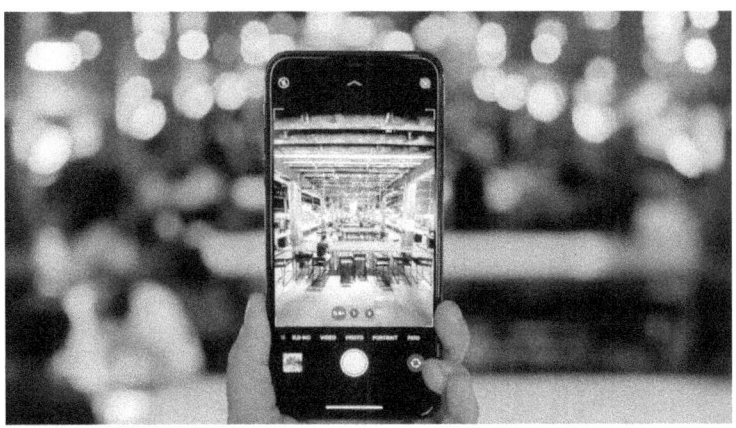

iPhone 12 Pro Camera Modes

Apple's iPhone 12 Pro comes with some changes in the features of the new camera app compared to other iPhones using iOS 14 and later. It comes with new controls, a way to move between the different cameras, and other features like quick video and more. This updated camera app interface can display an entire field of view captured by the camera's ultra-wide lens even though when it is the standard wide-angle lens that is being used in taking the photoshoot. Toggling between each of these modes is easily done by simply tapping and swiping relevant sections of the camera app.

To select a mode for shooting, simply swipe left or right across the screen or swipe down or up when holding the phone horizontally. Once a mode is selected, it will appear in yellow while the others will remain white.

The iPhone 12 Pro Camera app has six modes for shooting different photography and video modes. The modes include:

- Time-Lapse
- Slo-Mo
- Video
- Photo
- Portrait
- Pano

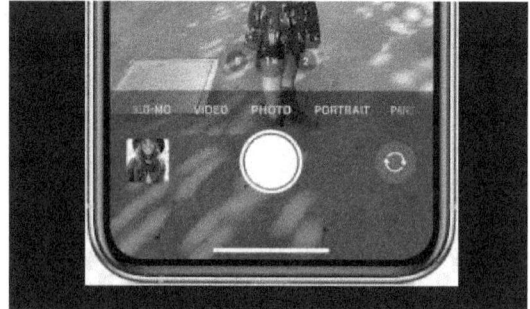

Figure 21: iPhone 12 Pro Photography Modes

Photo Mode

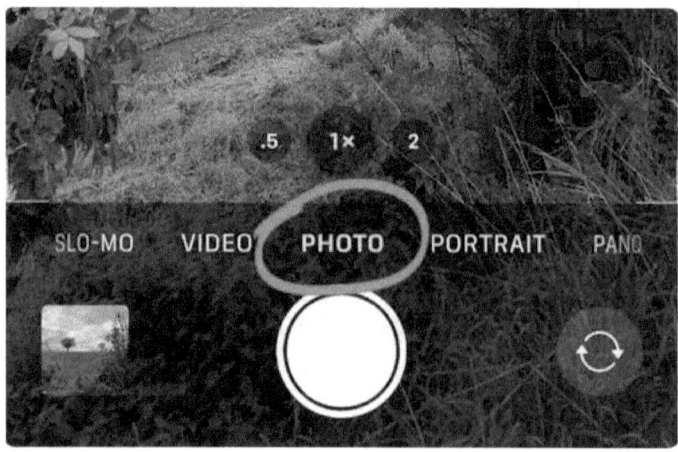

Figure 22: Photo Mode of iPhone 12 Pro

The default mode on the iPhone 12 Pro camera app is usually the Photo mode. This is also probably the most frequently used mode on the iPhone camera app because people tend to take a lot of still pictures with their phones compared to other photographic functions on the phone. It is used to capture normal still images.

Portrait Mode

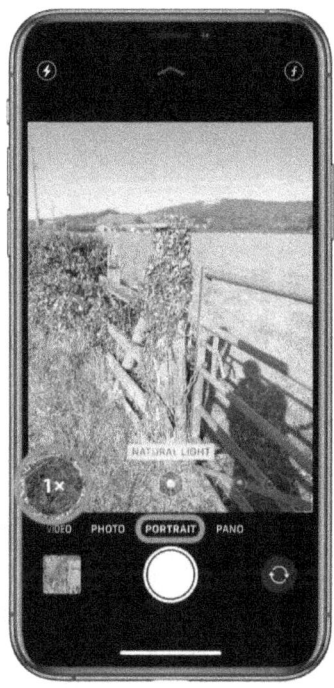

Figure 23: Portrait Mode of iPhone 12 Pro

To the right of the Photo mode on the iPhone 12 Pro Camera app is the Portrait mode. This feature is a handy one for shooting highly professional portrait photos with the iPhone as well as in creating beautiful background blur behind photoshoots.

Compared to the iPhone 7 Plus, 8 Plus, X, XS, XS Max, and iPhone XR which only allowed the use of their 2x telephoto camera when taking a portrait mode photo, the iPhone 12 Pro enables users to choose between the wide and telephoto lens for their portrait mode shots.

As expected, each of these modes produces an effect that is different from the other with the wide camera able to take better portrait photos in low light compared to the other camera because of its faster f/1.8 aperture.

Portrait mode is perfect for shooting professional-looking portrait photos.

Pano Mode

Next to the portrait mode is the Pano mode on the right. This mode is used to capture super-wide landscapes and cityscape pictures, including photos that are panoramic to capture more of the scenes.

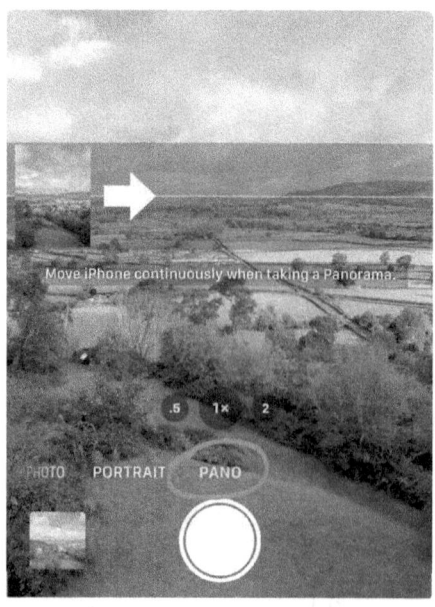

Figure 24: Pano Mode of iPhone 12 Pro

To use the Pano mode, you first tap the shutter button and then start moving the iPhone across the scene in the direction indicated by the arrow. As soon as you capture the parts of the scene you want to be captured, you can then tap the shutter button again to complete the shooting process.

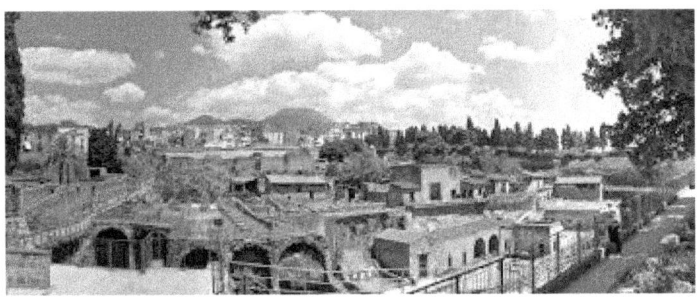

Figure 25: Photoshoot from Pano Mode

Video Mode

To the immediate left of the photo mode on the camera app is the video mode. This mode is used in the shooting of high-quality video footage. To use this feature, you start by tapping the red Record button to begin recording a video and tapping it again to stop its recording.

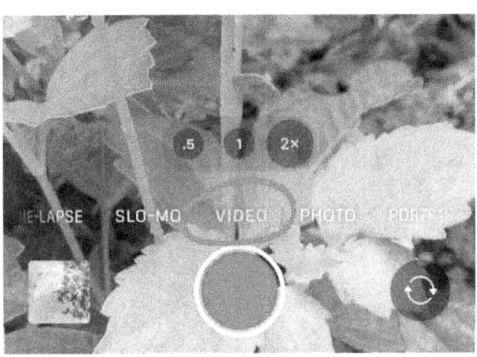

Figure 26: iPhone 12 Pro Video Mode

Slo-Mo Mode

Next to the video mode is the Slo-Mo mode used in capturing amazing slow-motion videos of fast-moving subjects like someone or an object running, flying, jumping, or moving.

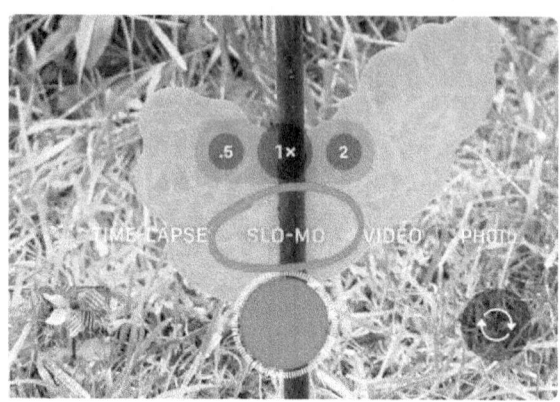

Figure 27: iPhone 12 Pro Slo-Mo Mode

As is common with other camera modes, you also have to tap the red Record button to begin recording a So-Mo and another tap to stop its recording.

Time-Lapse Mode

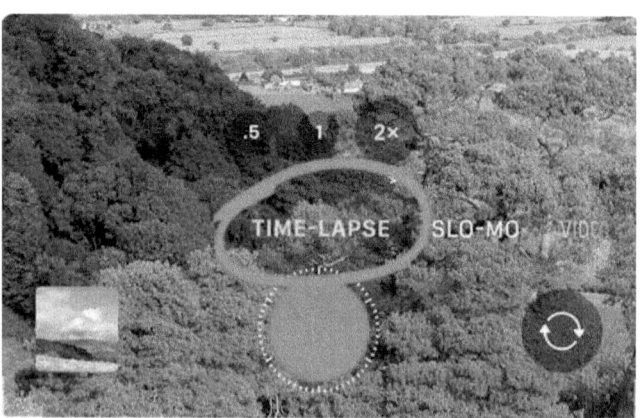

Figure 28: Time-Lapse Mode

Another essential camera mode of the iPhone 12 Pro camera app is the Time-Lapse Mode. This mode performs a function that is opposite of the Slo-Mo. It does this by creating a sped-up time-lapse video.

For Time-lapse, you also have to tap the red Record button to begin recording your time-lapse. To end the recording, all you have to do is to tap it again.

This feature is a fantastic way of hastening up slow-moving scenes like burning candles, clouds, or sunset.

Exploring The iPhone 12 Pro Lenses

The iPhone 12 Pro has three rear-facing lenses that include the Wide lens, an Ultra-Wide lens, and the telephoto lens, with each of them having different functions and specific uses. The Wide Lens is the iPhone 12 Pro's standard lens and has a relatively wide angle for viewing. Compared to the wide lens, the ultra-Wide lens gives users a much wider view field that users can use in capturing a lot more of any given scene, which makes it very useful in capturing wide architectural landscapes and nature pictures. It's equally great for capturing group pictures when you want more people to fit into the frame as well as interior shots where you want more parts of the scene captured.

The Telephoto lens, on the other hand, is beneficial for shots you want to zoom in to get a closer view. It is ideal for situations where you are unable to physically get close to the subject you want to capture.

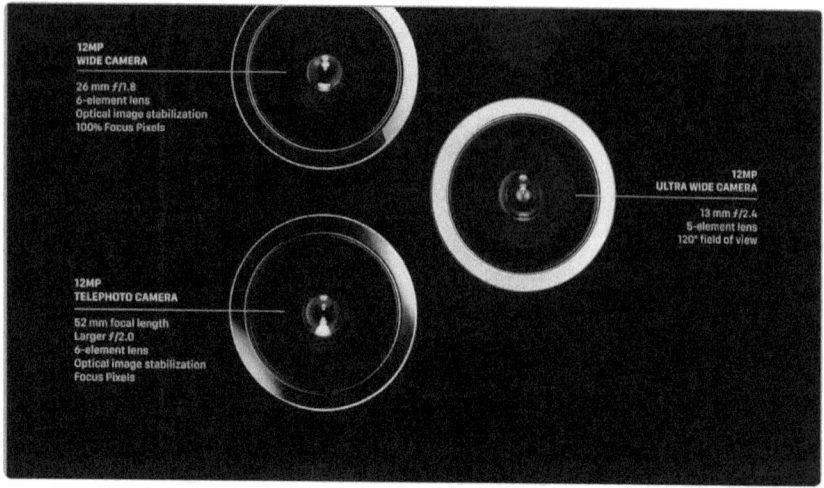

Figure 29: iPhone 12 Pro Camera Lenses

To compare the images from the different types of lenses, you will need to take pictures with the different lenses and to see the output of each of them.

Switching Between the Lenses

When it comes to videos, one of the coolest things you can do is to switch between different lenses while shooting, it is as easy as simply tapping the Zoom icons at the bottom of the viewfinder.

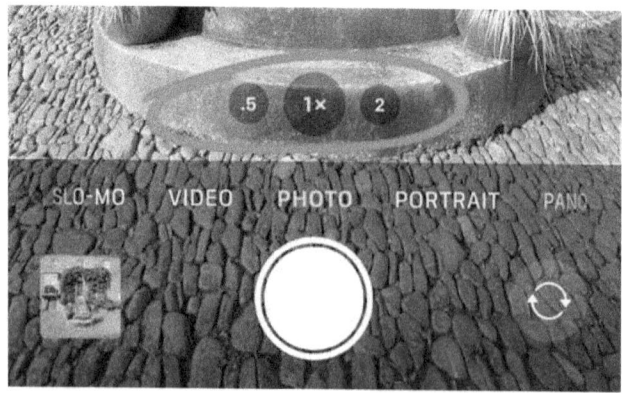

Figure 30: Wide Angle, Ultra-Wide, and Telephoto Lenses Selection

Switching to the Standard Wide-Angle Lens

To use the standard wide lens on any of the applicable modes like the photo mode, video mode, or pano mode, you simply tap the 1x under the viewfinder. Usually, this will be the default mode of the camera app.

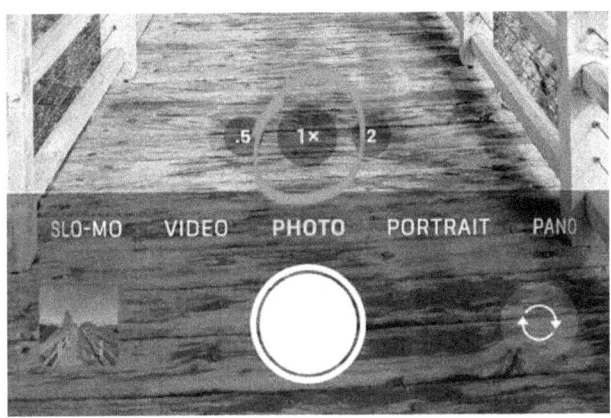

Figure 31: Standard Wide-Angle Lens Selection

Switching to the Ultra-Wide-Angle Lens

The ultra-wide-angle lens is useful for expanding the field of view of the camera for the scene where pictures are to be shot. To switch to the Ultra-Wide lens, simply tap the 0.5x.

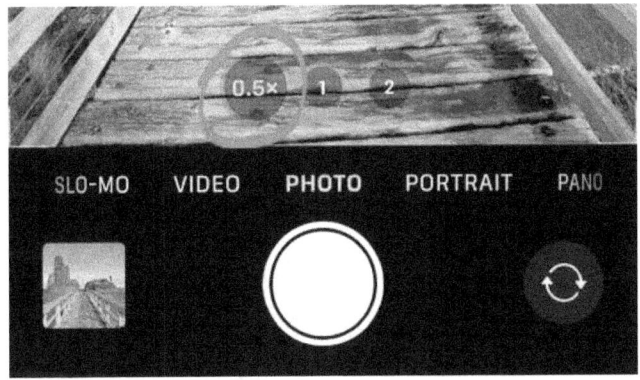

Figure 32: Ultra-Wide-Angle Lens Selection

Switching to the Telephoto Lens

The telephoto lens is useful in narrowing down the field of view of the camera lens by zooming in on the subject that the iPhone 12 Pro and 12 Prowant to shoot. The telephoto lens is the major difference between the iPhone 12 and iPhone 12 Pro. To switch the iPhone 12 Pro to the telephoto lens, simply tap the 2x icon below the viewfinder.

When you're using the 1x Wide lens or 2x Telephoto lens to shoot a scene, it will display a wider view of the scene outside of the frame. This will enable you to have an idea of what can be captured if you were to zoom out.

You can also get the zoom wheel to appear by holding down on any of the Zoom (0.5x, 1x, or 2x) icons.

The zoom wheel is very useful in choosing granular values different from the three fixed standard values and also shows the equivalent focal length in a 35mm film.

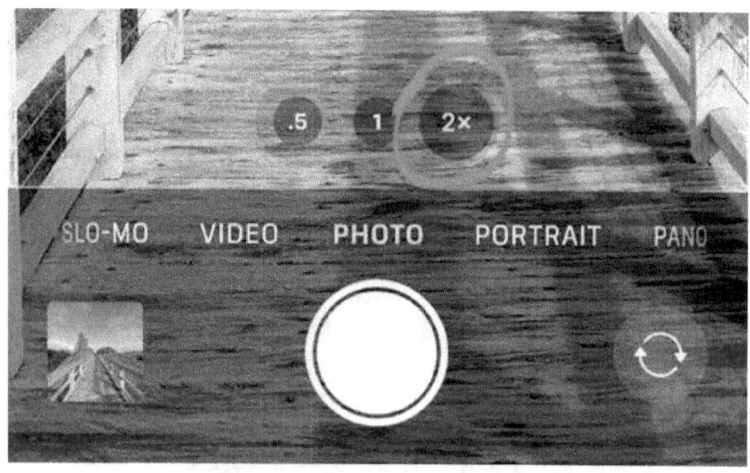

Figure 33: Telephoto Lens Selection

The zoom wheel allows you to zoom anywhere from 0.5x to 10x. By dragging the wheel towards the left or right, transiting between the different zoom levels can be achieved. For a lot of people, using the standard values of 0.5x, 1x, and 2x is usually sufficient for them because any zoom outside these three standard values will force the iPhone 12 Pro camera to use its digital zoom feature which tends to result in much more inferior image quality that does not do enough justice to the iPhone 12 Pro camera capabilities. The fixed focal length values of 0.5x, 1x, and 2x built-into the cameras make use of the full optical quality of the three iPhone 12 Pro's lenses to produce high-quality images.

Fine Tuning the zoom in and Out

The iPhone 12 Pro gives users an added advantage of making use of all the three 12 megapixels lenses that it comes with, including their respective zoom levels.

The control of the iPhone 12 Pro Camera's zoom is different from other previous versions. On the iPhone, you will find two (0.5x and 1x) buttons that you can tap, whereas the iPhone 12 Pro has a third button for its 2x zoom.

The iPhone 12 Pro uses 1x for the default camera wide lens, whereas the ultra-wide camera uses the 0.5x option from the possible three options available when you attempt using the zoom.

To zoom on the iPhone 12 Pro

- Tap on the camera app to open it

- Select either the 0.5x, 1x, or the 2x buttons on the camera app to jump to that zoom level, or you can tap and hold any of the options to open up the zoom wheel

Drag the dial that appears so that you can transition between the other cameras and zoom more smoothly

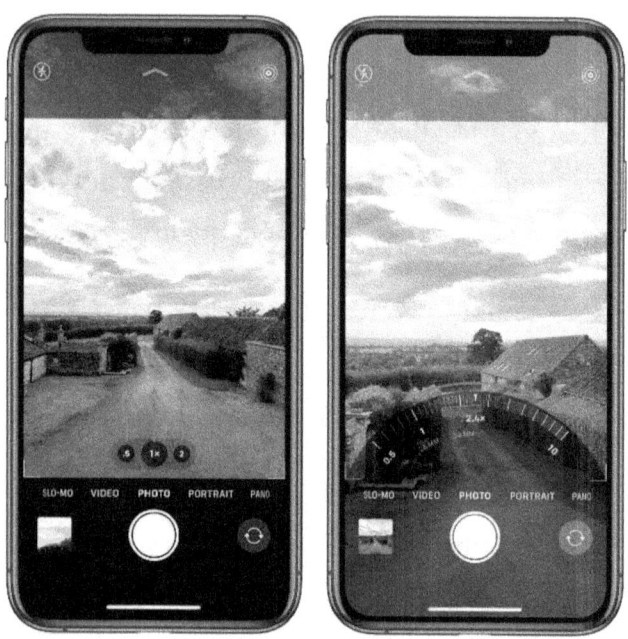

Figure 34: Zooming Images Using Presets or Zoom Wheel

You use this option to select intermediate zoom levels rather than specific values and also expose the equivalent focal length in 35mm film.

If you have used any of the custom zoom levels, it is possible to move back to 1x by just pressing the center button.

Another way to Operate the Zoom Feature

- Tap the camera app to launch the app

- Pinch and zoom with two of your fingers on the screen and adjust the zoom
- Switch between the lenses and select your preferred one

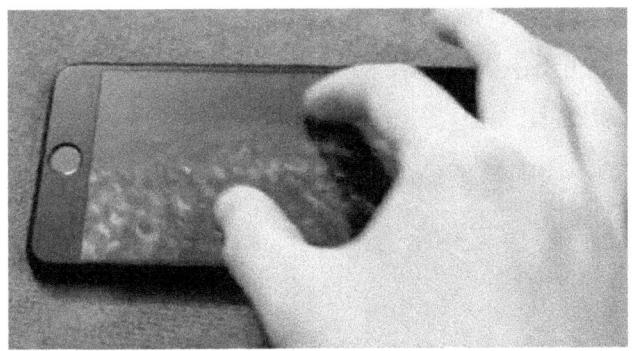

Figure 35: Zooming by Pinching with Two Fingers

NB: This option does not open the focal length wheel

You can return to the 1x zoom at any time by pressing the center button if you have previously changed to a custom zoom level when playing around with the zoom feature.

Zoom Out Photos After Shooting

The iPhone 12 Pro also has a hidden feature that is possible because of the ultrawide camera, that is the possibility of zooming out on a photo captured by any of the other two lenses to get a wider picture frame after you've taken it. With this feature, more people who were originally not captured in a group photograph can be included because the ultra-wide pictures tend to keep a copy of every shot taken so that you can bring such persons initially missed back into the shot using the crop tool on the Photos app.

Expanding your Photoshoot Scene

If you are passionate about phone photography, then you must turn on the feature called "View outside the frame" in the camera settings. This allows you to see the parts of the photo that you are not going to capture. When you're using the telephoto lens, it shows you a sort of preview of what the wide lens will look like, it also gives you a preview of the ultra-wide lens when you're using the wide lens. This makes sure that you know you're using the right lens and not zooming in unnecessarily.

Introducing the LIDAR Sensor

The iPhone 12 Pro has a new special sensor, called the 'LIDAR' sensor, which enables the camera to take better night photos and even better photos in daylight, but that's not what we are talking about. With the LIDAR sensor, you can do a bunch of other stuff on your iPhone.

Apple is not the only company to make use of LIDAR, as a matter of fact, LIDAR is an innovative tech sprouting up in a lot of tech applications. Just like in the proximity sensing abilities of bats, it's used for cars that are self-driving or assisted driving. The robotics and drone fields also make use of it a lot.

It does this by sending lasers to ping off on objects you focus on, after which it then returns to the source of the laser. The length of time it takes to return is then used to compute the distance between the object and the laser source.

There is an app made by Apple themselves, called "Measure", and what it does is to make use of the LIDAR sensor, and it quite accurately measures how far a person or an object is from you.

You can pretty much point the camera in the app at anybody and the sensor will measure how close or far the person is from you. Of course, it does not work for objects that are too far away, typically about 5m. It's quite helpful and can help to replace the measuring tape to measure the length of the distance of specific items and for a lot of stuff around you.

Using the Volume Buttons as a Shutter

You can take a picture with the iPhone 12 Pro using the volume button instead of the shutter button. As with many things on the iPhone 12 Pro, this is essentially simple to do. This shortcut according to Apple is referred to as 'Quick takes'. These quick takes are listed below:

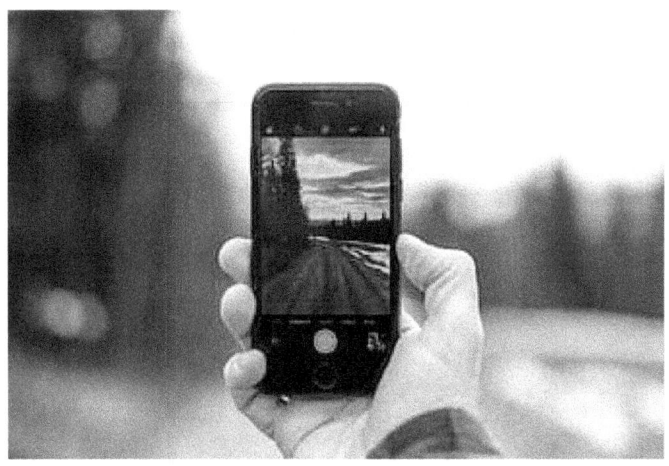

Figure 36: Taking a Picture with the Volume Button

When you open your camera app, just press any of the volume buttons and your shutter will shoot the picture.

Though this trick is common in every smartphone, Apple has done something interesting. If you long-press and hold any of the volume buttons the camera will start recording a video for you. Recording stops as soon as you release the button.

Quick Take Using the iPhone 12 Pro Volume Button

- Tap Camera app to launch it
- Focus the camera on the subject you want to take
- Tap the up-volume button to take a picture
- Launch the Camera app by tapping on it. The default mode when you launch the Camera app will be the Photo mode
- Direct the camera to focus on the subject whose picture is to be taken
- When the subject is in focus, tap the shutter to snap the picture

Taking Pictures with the Rear Cameras

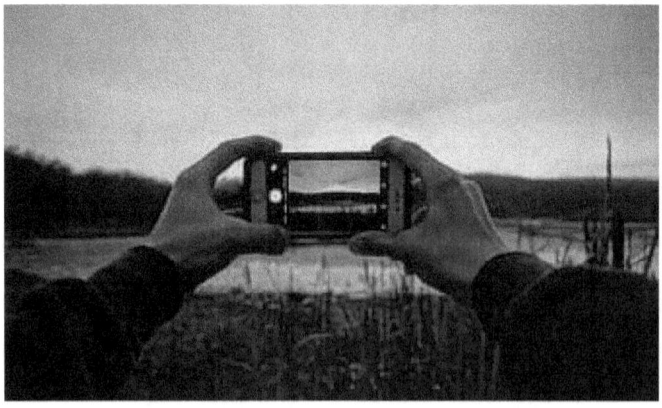

Figure 37: Capture Important Moments with the iPhone 12 Pro

How to Record Videos

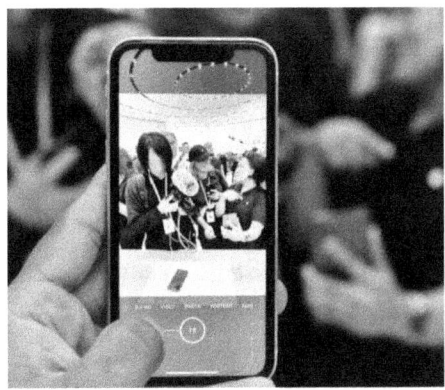

Figure 38: Capture Important Moments Using the Video Recorder

- Launch the Camera app by tapping on it.
- Change from the default Photo mode to Video mode by tapping on the video option beside the photo option above the shutter button
- Tap the Record button to start the recording
- Tap the Record button again to stop recording when done

Recording a Video Between Photos Using QuickTake

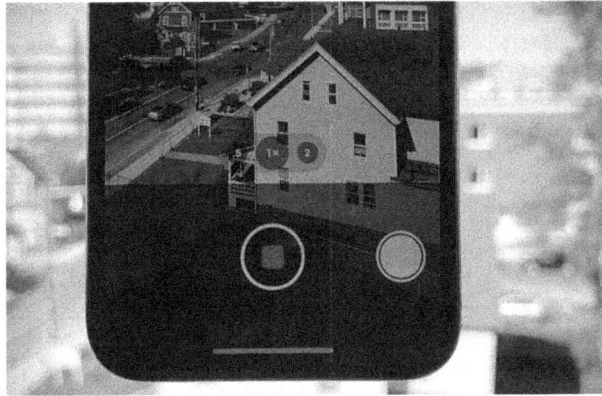

Figure 39: Switching Quickly from Still Pictures to Video Recording

If you have ever wished there was a way to instantly switch from capturing a still picture to start recording a video without having to change modes just like in a Snapchat story or Instagram story, then the QuickTake feature is for you. To achieve that on older iPhones will typically involve switching to Video mode and pressing the shutter button to begin recording. On the iPhone 12 Pro, you can shoot a video and still stay in Photo mode.

This feature is very simple to activate and use, although slightly different from the way lower versions of the iPhone 12 Pro achieve it. QuickTake can be used on both front and rear cameras, even though users have to pay attention to the aspect ratio. QuickTake will always inherit the aspect ratio of the photograph being taken, so a photograph set to 4:3 will use that same setting for the QuickTake. If you prefer your video to be 16:9 instead, you will need to set the photo aspect ratio accordingly. To record with the QuickTake, pay attention to the following steps.

- Hold the shutter button to begin recording the QuickTake video while still in Photo mode. The shutter button will turn red. And you'll see the video timer at the top of the screen.
- Remove your hands from the shutter to stop the QuickTake video recording, and you can continue taking photos.

To release your hands to keep capturing still pictures or performing other activities, it is better to lock the QuickTake while the video recording is ongoing.

- To achieve this, slide the Shutter button to the right of the screen to expose both the record and shutter buttons below the frame

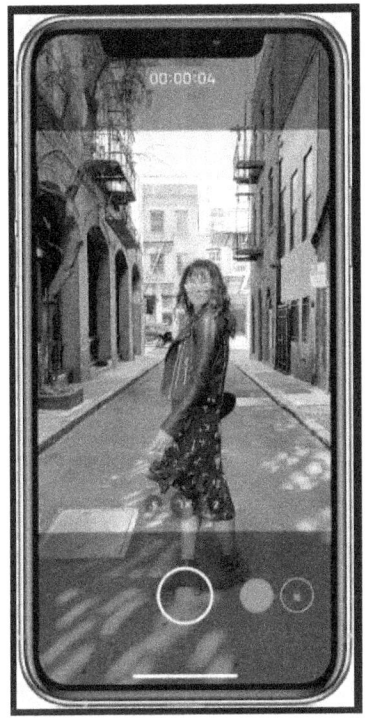

Figure 40: QuickTake Timer

- When you lock the video recording, a white shutter button appears at the bottom right corner of the screen. The shutter button can then be used to continue taking still images, while the QuickTake video recording is still ongoing.

The Record button can be used to stop the ongoing recording by simply tapping it.

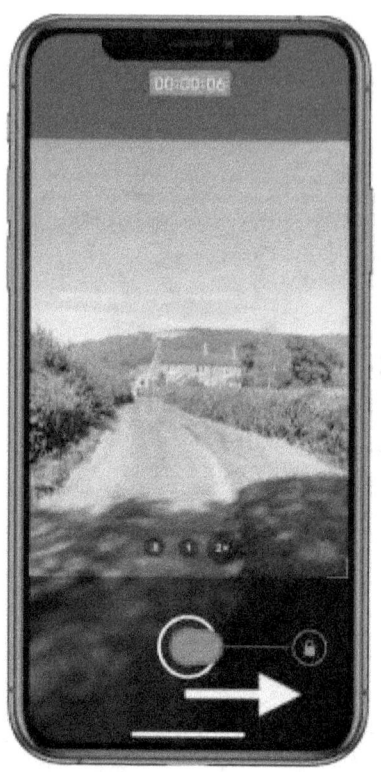

Figure 41: Locking the QuickTake Video

This is a really cool feature that allows users to both shoot videos and photos at the same time. It is important to note that the resolution of the images can be slightly lower than normal, but nowhere near being a poor-quality image.

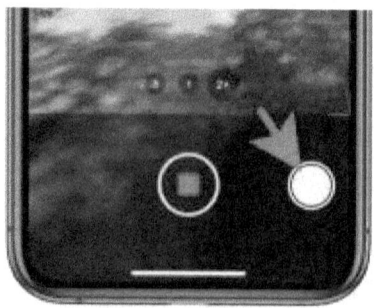

Figure 42: White Shutter Button to Continue Pictures

Taking Burst Photos

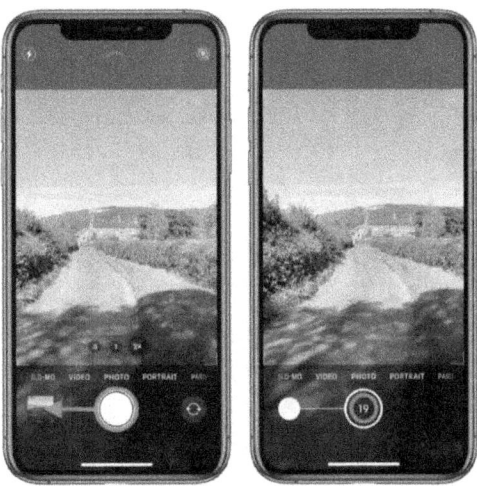

Figure 43: Using the Burst Features of the iPhone 12 Pro

Imagine you want a precise picture of you taken midair when you leap off the ground and want the timing to be gotten right, so that the image comes out crisp and not blurry, or you want to take a shot of you running, or a picture of a moving vehicle, previous versions of the iPhone have customarily used the burst function to achieve this. The burst mode is a fantastic iPhone tool for capturing subjects that are in motion. So, if you have difficulty shooting moving objects and you know it can be a struggle to press the shutter button at the precise moment this burst mode feature is definitely for you.

In earlier versions of the iPhone that also had the burst function like the iPhone 12 Pro, you only needed to press and hold the shutter button, and the device will keep capturing the pictures for as long as the finger remains on the screen.

Well, for the new iPhone 12 Pro, that function is now used for the QuickTake function. In this recent release, the burst currently requires some more steps to achieve compared to just holding the shutter in the photo mode of previous versions.

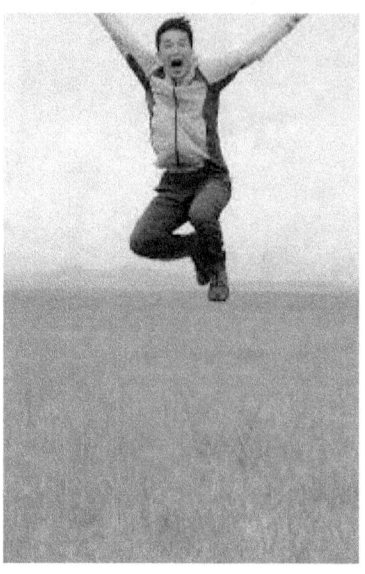

Figure 44: Capture Image Mid Air with Burst Feature

When you take a shot in burst mode, multiple photos are taken every second to capture the subject as it moves across the scene until you release your finger so that you are able to select the best shot from the burst with the option to discard the others. The number of photos taken within the burst is indicated by the number inside the shutter.

To take a burst on the iPhone 12 Pro, follow these simple steps.

- Launch the Camera app on your iPhone
- Press on the shutter button

- Then quickly swipe to the left towards the photo's stack of thumbnails if you are taking a vertical photo or swipe down for horizontal photos

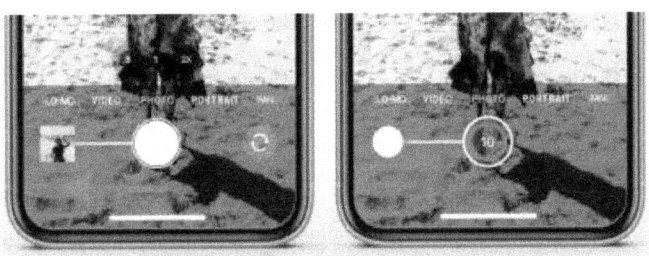

Figure 45: Shooting a Burst Photo

Ensure the shutter button is not red. If it is red, that means you may have held your finger too long on the shutter causing the phone to think you want to record a video. If that is the case, you have to start all over.

If you did it correctly, the shutter cycle would move in the direction of your finger to indicate the starting of the burst. To end the burst, simply remove your finger from the screen.
When the burst photo shooting has been completed, you can then open the burst thumbnail in the Photos app. The burst photos can be identified from the thumbnail by their stacked images. It is from there that you now tap and select the Relevant you want to keep. Tap Done when through to keep only the selected photos. The selected pictures are then saved to your photo library, and the others are deleted.

Setting Up Photo Capture Outside of the Frame

Capturing images outside a photo frame with the ultra-wide uses a function referred to as composition. Composition is an important feature that differentiates a well-taken picture from an ordinary snapshot.

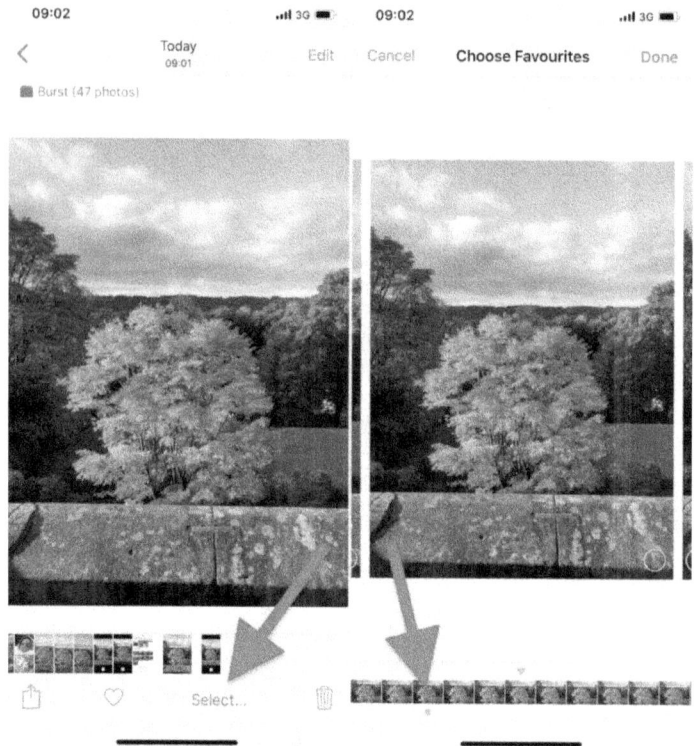

Figure 46: Burst Mode Picture Selection

If, for example, you want to take a shot, but there are persons on the edge of the frame not captured, rather than zoom in, you can instead recover a slightly wider field of view by utilizing the cameras on the iPhone 12 Pro by turning on the composition setting.

To set the phone to be able to take pictures outside the frame, you can follow these steps.

- Tap to launch the Settings App on your iPhone

- Select and tap Camera

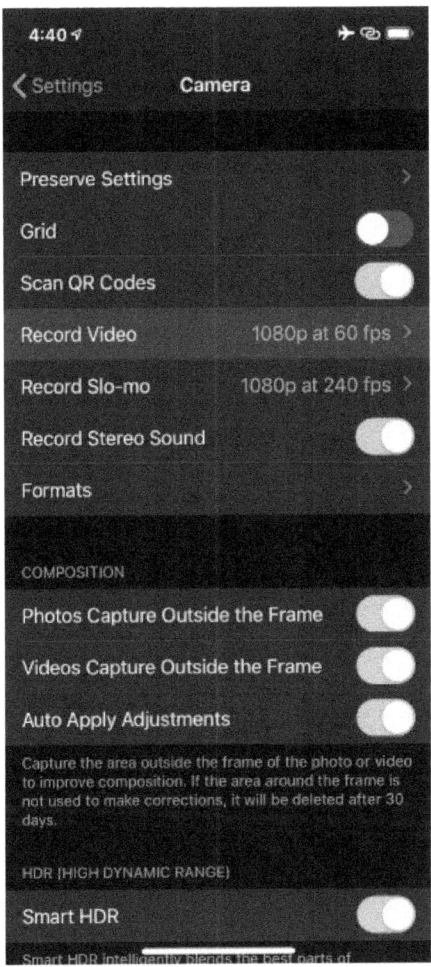

Figure 47: Configuring Composition on the iPhone 12 Pro

- Toggle the switch close to the Photos Capture Outside the Frame and Videos Capture Outside the Frame to switch on the iPhone's function of being able to capture images and videos outside the current frame

- Next, tap the switch beside Auto Apply Adjustment so that composition adjustments can be applied to any of your photoshoots

It is noteworthy to know that enabling and disabling this function can only be done by going into the Settings app and not the Camera app. So, go to Settings -> Camera -> Composition, where you can set the three toggles. You will notice that separate toggles are used to control the outside the frame switches for photos and videos and another switch for Auto-Apply Adjustments.

A valuable note about this feature is that when you capture photos or videos outside the standard frame of your camera, you will be required to save the images using Apple's higher efficient HEIC and HEVC image instead of JPG.

Taking Advantage of Outside the Frame

While it is possible to use the wide-angle shot when taking a picture, it is also sometimes possible to have taken a picture around the active viewfinder, only to discover when you want to edit or use the image that some aspect of the background was cut out and not captured in the standard frame.

The good news is that if you have set the outside the frame feature in the iPhone settings, then you can nevertheless have access to the ultra-wide-angle shot because the iPhone ensures that it takes more than one shot when a picture is being taken.

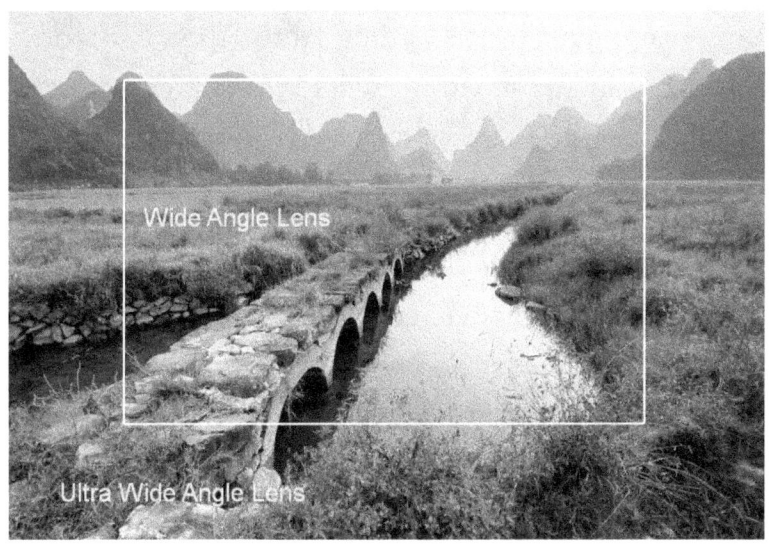

Figure 48: Utilizing the Ultra and Wide-angle-lens

Therefore, if you took a photo, but a person on the edge of the frame isn't captured, you can then edit the photo by zooming out to see a wider shot of the image which may now have the person that was left out in the standard frame because the ultra-wide lens would have also taken a copy of the picture. It should be noted that this can only happen if you turned on Photo Capture Outside the Frame the phone's composition setting and works for both photos and videos. To take advantage of this feature, you can follow the simple steps below.

- Tap to launch the Photos app on your iPhone 12 Pro
- Tap to open the video or photo you want to edit
- Tap Edit. If the picture has data from outside the frame that can be edited, you will notice a rangefinder icon with a star
- Use the crop tool to extend the edges surrounding the present frame to expose more parts of the photo or videos

- You can equally use the Auto-Apply to do this automatically for situations where the app can detect faces or subjects that were not captured
- Tap Done after the edit

If you capture images outside the standard frame, you have to note these pictures can get deleted after 30 days if they are unused within that time frame even though the image from the standard lens can nonetheless exist long after the picture had been taken.

Although this feature is simple to use, many users sometimes find it confusing to use. Some captured pictures sometimes do not display other aspects of the photos when zoomed in, even though the square box is used to indicate that more information exists outside the frame.

It turns out that there are two different ways of accessing the information captured outside the frame. However, if trying to zoom out on a photo doesn't work, you can try selecting the Crop tool as before, then tap on the three-dot icon at the top right corner, and then tap Use Content Outside the Frame. For photos that have previously been cropped and straightened, there is likely to be a warning message that your previous cropping is about to be reset, tap to accept the warning so that you are now able to edit the ultrawide shot.

Scanning QR Codes with your iPhone

Scanning QR codes are now super simple and easy. You can switch on the option in the camera setting called "Scan QR codes", and your camera will automatically detect and scan the

QR code for you, without you asking the camera to do it. It is quite useful, as we often need to scan QR codes to access certain websites or get product information.

Figure 49: Scanning a QR Code

Expanding the Capability of the Front Camera

Did you know that the front camera on the iPhone 12 Pro can switch between 8MP to 12MP whenever you want? The camera is 12MP, but by default, it is set at 8MP capacity, you can tap on the little zoom out button on the bottom, or if you rotate your screen, you will see that the camera angle gets wider, and that is the full capacity of the 12 MP camera. The option to switch is useful if you like to take close-up selfies or want to focus on a particular part of your face. The wider mode is great for groupies, or if you want to show some of the backgrounds behind you.

Mirroring Front Camera

When you take a selfie, it usually flips the photo so that the scene looks different from how it is in reality, and this is because the front camera flips the image it takes. This is particularly obvious with text on a signpost. A lot of people find this to be particularly annoying and do all they can to flip it back.

Well, not anymore, you can now preserve any text so that it shows up in its original form because you now can access the setting called" Mirror front camera" which enables your camera to take the photo as you see it on the screen, without flipping it to look accurate. It is a great feature because most people like the photo as it looks on the screen and not flipped the other way.

Chapter 4

Manipulating Images on iPhone 12 Pro

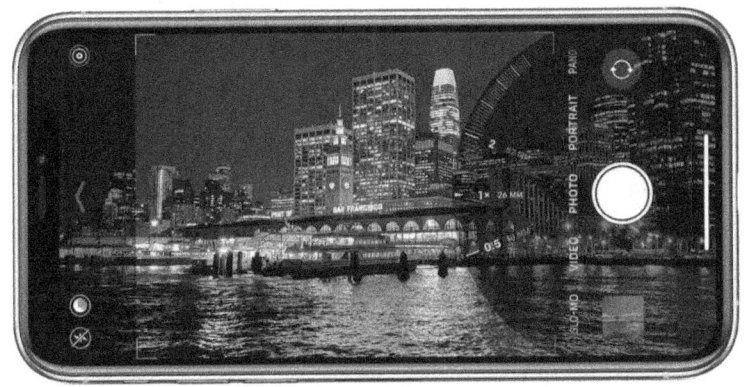

For those who prefer to use the iPhone's native app in editing photos rather than utilizing expensive editing programs like Photoshop, the instructions below are useful. The iPhone 12 Pro has powerful photo editing tools that can be used to edit photos for cropping, filtering, adjusting color balance, and other simple essential functions.

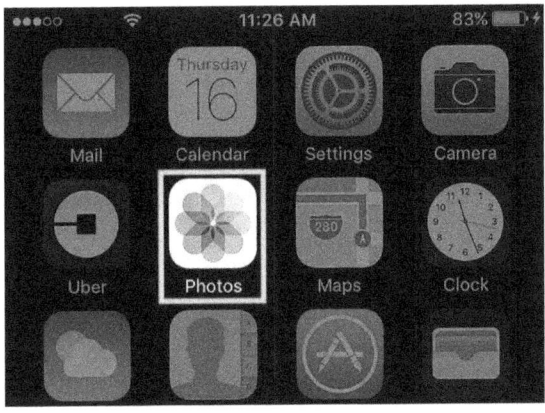

Figure 50: iPhone Photos App

Editing a Photo or Video

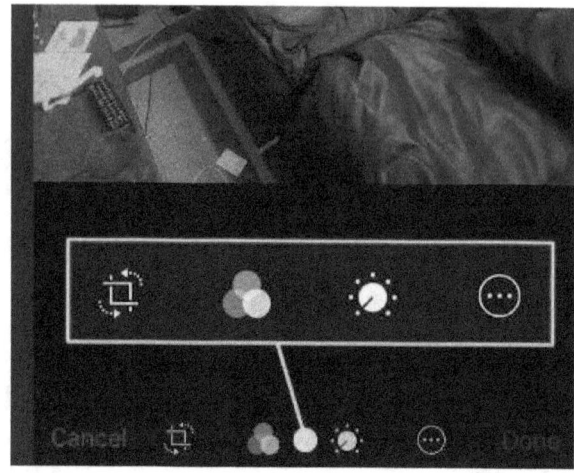

Figure 51: Locating the Edit Button on the Photos App

- Tap the Photos app to launch it
- Tap the photo or video thumbnail you intend to edit to open it
- Tap Edit, then swipe left below the photo to view the buttons for editing effects like crop, brilliance, highlights, and exposure.
- Tap a button and then drag the slider to make the changes required
- The outline displayed around the button is used to indicate the effects of the adjustments made as they either increase or decrease

Before and After Effects of Photo Edits

With the Photos app still opened, after the changes have been applied, you can see the effects of your actions on the subject by performing the following steps.

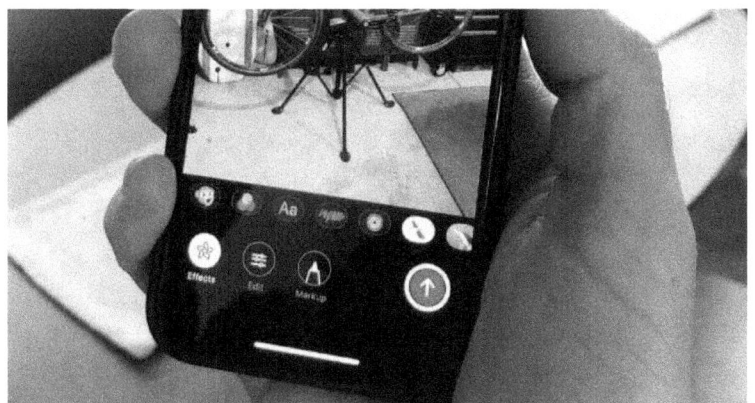

Figure 52: Locating the Effects Button on the Photos App

- Tap the effect button to show the before effects shots of the photo and the aftereffect shots of the picture.
- Tap the photo to toggle from the original version of the picture to the edited version
- Tap Done to accept the changes and Cancel to discard the changes

Take Screenshots

Taking screenshots on the iPhone 12 Pro is one feature that many users find very useful because it allows them to document activities or messages on the phone for future references. To do that, you have to follow these simple steps.

- Press and hold the Volume up button with the Side button at the same time before releasing them quickly.
- The thumbnail of your screenshot will appear at the lower-left corner of your screen
- Tap that thumbnail to effect minor changes and edits
- To share the screenshot, press and hold the thumbnail

- However, if you are unsatisfied with it and perhaps want to discard it, you can swipe it to the left of the screen to do so, otherwise, you can save it

Knowing the Different Cropping Options

Many users of the iPhone 12 Pro cameras are likely to be social media savvy and may not want to be restricted in terms of the photo ratio or sizes and want to be able to adjust pictures after they have been taken. Fortunately, the iPhone 12 Pro allows that to happen.

- Tap to open the iPhone 12's Pro Photos app
- Tap a photo or video thumbnail of what you desire to edit
- Tap Edit and select the crop tool, you can identify it by its square icon with arrows surrounding it

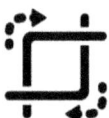

- To crop manually, drag the corners of the rectangle surrounding it by closing in on the areas of the photo you want to keep. You can also pinch the picture and drag to obtain the corresponding effect
- To crop to a standard preset ratio, tap the preset button, and select any of the preset options like the Square, 5:4, 3:2, 5:3,4:3, and 8:10. You can use 16:9 and 7:5 for panoramic photos even though 1:1 is more popular with Instagram users
- To rotate an image, tap the rounded square with a rotating arrow on top to rotate the photo by 90 degrees

- Select the flip button to flip the image horizontally when you want to flip an image around
- Tap Done to save changes and Cancel to discard changes.

Straightening and Adjusting Perspective

- Tap the Photos app to launch it
- Tap a photo or video thumbnail of what you desire to edit
- Tap Edit followed by the crop button
- Select an effect button for straightening and adjusting the horizontal and vertical perspective
- For photos captured by the ultra-wide camera, aspects of the picture outside the frame can be automatically used to make changes to alignments and perspective. A blue Auto icon that appears above the photo is used to indicate an automatic adjustment was applied
- Use the slider to adjust the effect by sliding across the slider
- Watch the displayed yellow outline around the button to monitor the effectiveness of your adjustments on the photo
- Tap the button to switch between the original and the edited effect to observe the impact of your changes
- Tap Done to save your changes or Cancel to discard your change

How to Use Filters Correctly

The default camera app on the iPhone 12 Pro already comes with several basic filters on it. They are quite limited, but it's still useful since you can quickly brighten up or dim down your picture. You can also go to the settings and keep a specific filter as default if you like. There are many third-party apps as well, which you can download from the AppStore, which gives you a larger variety of options for filters.

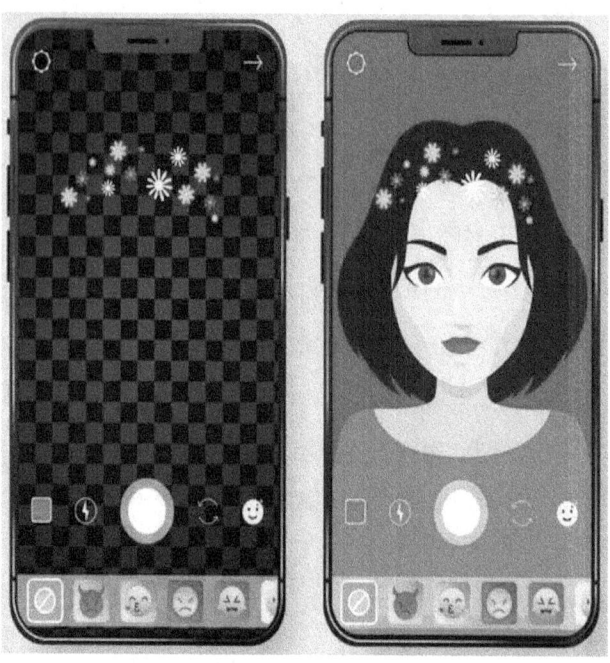

Figure 53: Enhancing a Photo with Filters

Using filters can be fun and can change your photos to look unique and have a different feel. Learning how to use appropriate filters is the first step of learning photo editing.

Filters generally come in three categories; they are either warm, cool, or neutral. Warm filters generally have a yellow or orange tint. It enhances earthy tones and mutes the more vibrant ones.

Cool filters usually have a bluish or a purple cast, and generally, enhance more vibrant tones while keeping the earthy and yellow tones rather muted. Neutral filters are filters such as greyscale, black and white, vibrant, and many more. Neutral filters simply enhance or dim down the overall colors on a photo.

As you can already tell, a warm filter is for sunny days and a cool filter is for cloudy or snowy days. However, that is just a generalization, there is more to filters than just warm and cool tones.

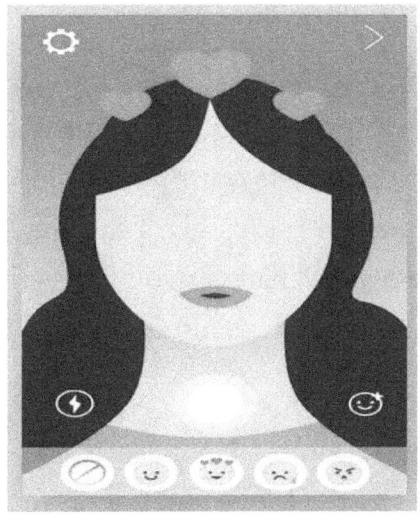

Figure 54: Post Shooting Filters on Photos

Some filters change certain colors to look like something else, for example, if you apply a very warm filter on a picture with a lot of yellow, the yellow will start looking orange.

However, if you apply a cool filter, the yellow will turn more brownish. When we take photos of nature, one of the main problems we face is that the colors in the photo look different than the colors in real life. This is where a good filter can save the day. Since filters are pre-made, you can try out different ones before you even take the picture.

However, if you forget, you can always add a filter later on by simply tapping on the "edit" button.

Filters are not limited to landscape photography. You can learn how to use filters to color correct a person's skin tone or to adjust the warmth or coldness of a photo. Neutral filters such as greyscale can be used to make the picture look more subdued, brighter, or to change the mood of a photo. These are generally used to take aesthetically pleasing photos.

Filters are also great at producing more cinematic effects. Some apps offer filters that can turn your photo to look like a painting, while other filters can make it look like a cartoon, or an old movie, or a futuristic neon board. Whatever you fancy, there is a filter for it. You can access some of these filters on the camera inside the iMessage itself.

If you like taking Instagram worthy photos, then you must learn how to use filters correctly. It can make your feed looks like that of a celebrity or a professional photographer. Finally, all I can say is that filters are fun, so go try them out and see the magic for yourself.

Taking a Photo with a Filter

To use the filter feature of the iPhone 12 Pro to take pictures by adding filters at the point of taking the pictures by following these steps.

- Open the Camera app
- Choose Photo or Portrait mode
- Tap the arrow pointing up

- Tap the filter button
- Under the viewer, swipe the filters around from left to right to preview the effects
- Tap on any of them to select it

If, after taking the image with a predefined filter and you later do not like what you see, you can then use the Photo app on the iPhone to alter the preset of filter you applied to your image at any time without significantly affecting the quality of the picture.

The photo app on the iPhone does not, in this case, overlay the filter over the already existing one, instead, it replaces it so that you do not have a photograph with oversaturated unnatural colors.

Applying Filter Effects on a Photo

- Tap to launch the Photos app
- Tap a photo or video thumbnail to open the photo you want to edit

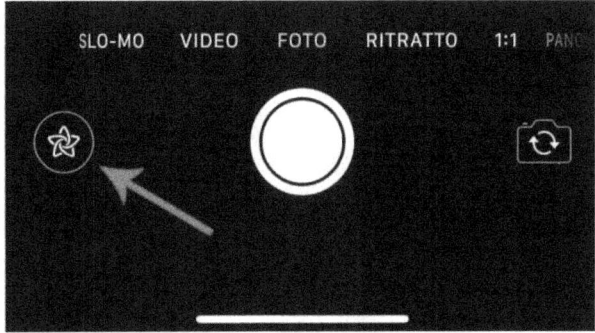

Figure 55: Selecting Options on the Camera App

- Tap Edit followed by the filter button 🔘 (three cycles arranged in a triangular format) to apply any of the filters you want
- Tap to select a filter and use the slider to adjust the effect of the filter
- Tap the photo to switch between the original and edited photo to monitor the differences so far
- Tap Done when satisfied with the outcome and Cancel to discard the changes

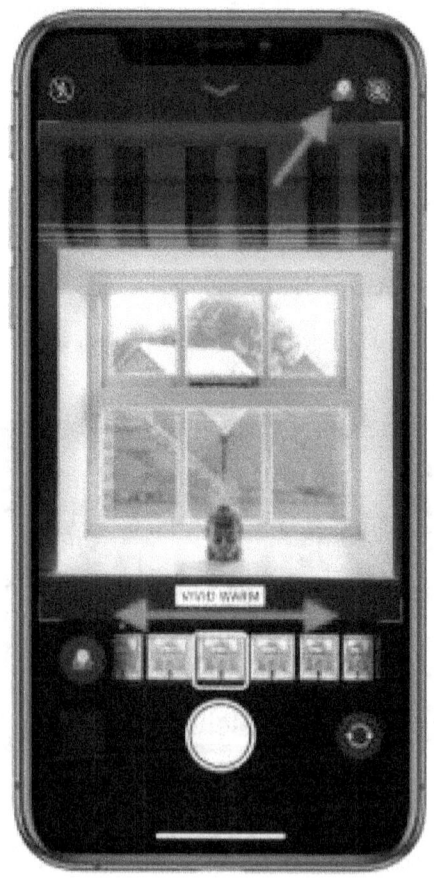

Figure 56: Applying Filters

The Filters icon grants you access to a wide range of preset filters you can use to change various outlooks of your image, depending on the filter selected, any of these filters can produce a unique effect on the images or photos they are applied to.

Photos can also have these filters applied or removed from them when pictures are edited in the Photos app. A lot of people find that it is simpler to capture a scene with no filter and have the filter applied later when processing the image.

When taking pictures without applying filters, it is important to ensure that the filter selected is the default.

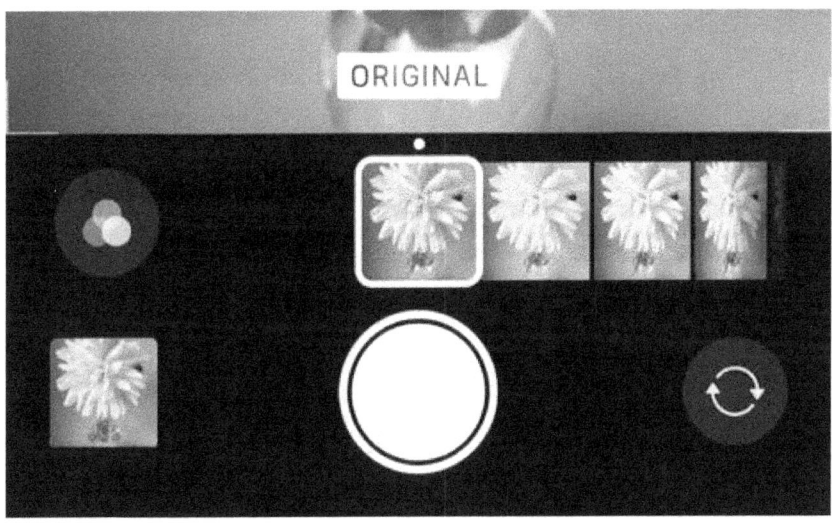

Figure 57: Using the Default Filter

Marking Up a Photo

- Tap the Photos app to open it
- Tap a photo you want to put annotations on
- Tap edit and tap the three dots at the top

- Select Markup Ⓐ.
- Use the different available drawing tools and colors to annotate the photo

Tap the plus sign to add more shapes and text

Trimming a Video

If you have a video to send via Messages or Mail but find that it is too long to send at once, you may want to only send some parts of the video instead. To do that, you can use the trim function to start and stop the video timing when you want to make the video shorter than the original version without using iMovie.

- Tap the Photos app to open it
- Tap the video thumbnail of the video you want to edit
- Tap Edit and drag either end of the frame viewer
- Release when satisfied with the trim
- Tap Done to accept changes or Cancel to discard

Reverting to an Original Photo or Video

Even after editing and saving the changes in a photo, you can revert to the original image by adopting these simple steps.

- Tap the Photo's App to launch it
- Tap the Photo or Video thumbnail to open the photo that was edited
- Tap Edit followed by Revert
- Select Revert to Original

Changing the Aspect Ratio

On the iPhone 12 Pro, it is quite easy to change the aspect ratios within a few seconds. To do that on the Camera app, look out for the carrot icon, and you will see the option of Aspect Ratio. Tap on that and choose an aspect ratio that is suitable for your picture. The allowed aspect ratios on the iPhones 12 Pro are 4:3, 16:9, and 1:1 square. Unlike some other previous versions of the iPhone, where users could only choose between the 4:3 aspect ratio (rectangle) and the 1:1 aspect ratio (Square), the iPhone 12 Pro groups the ratio settings into a single-mode, which also includes the new 16:9 aspect ratio. To change the aspect ratio, you can follow the steps below.

- Launch the Camera app
- Swipe up the screen to expose more of the Camera settings
- Tap the aspect ratio button (usually 4:3 by default)
- Select any of the available options to make it the new aspect ratio

Shooting with the Ultra-Wide Lens

- It is easy to shoot with the iPhone ultra-wide lens
- Tap to open the Camera app
- Tap the 1x button to switch over to the 0.5x ultra-wide lens
- You can now take your picture

Indicator for Camera Rolling

One of the newest things about the iPhone is the little green light on top of the phone. What is it you ask? Well, it is a simple LED light that tells you whenever the camera is open. As we all are more concerned about our security, this light will give you an indication whenever your camera is in use. This tiny light will come up whenever you turn your camera on. So, if for some reason, it is turned on when you're not in the camera app, you know that something else is using it so and you can check to see what app has turned it on.

Chapter 5

Additional Controls on the Camera App

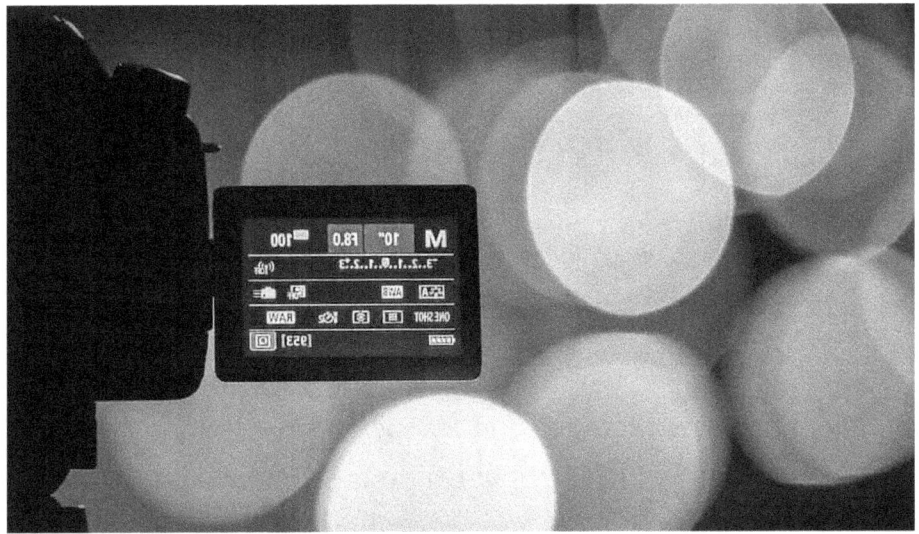

The iPhone 12 Pro Camera comes with many other hidden controls and settings that a user can manipulate. Whenever you notice a triangular arrow pointing upwards, you can swipe it up on the viewfinder to expose a new set of controls. Other controls like options for flash, night mode, live photos, and a few others are possible within these extra functions.

Learn to Take Great Selfies All by Yourself

The iPhone 12 Pro has three cameras at the back. 12MP telephoto lens, 12MP ultra-wide lens, and a 12MP wide-angle lens and also features a 12MP front-facing camera, which delivers really good quality crisp images just like the back cameras. This camera was especially put into place because of all the selfie lovers.

We all know how to take a basic selfie, just hold out the camera and shoot an image, but there is so much more to a selfie than what we usually know. You can use a stand and the self-timer to take photos of yourself that looks like it was taken by someone else. You can similarly use the back camera using a stand and take higher quality pictures.

This camera setup offers different modes that you can use to take great pictures, but you can also take selfies with them. As mentioned before, you will need a stand to take selfies with the back camera, but as long as you have that, it's very easy to capture beautiful self-portraits with all three lenses.

The telephoto lens provides you a super zoomed-in photo with great detail. If you want to show off your makeup skills, or your newly groomed beard, this lens can capture highly detailed facial features and make the photos look as though they are professionally taken.

The ultra-wide-angle mode allows you to take full pictures of a person even without going far away from the phone. This means you can easily take full pictures of yourself without the help of anyone. You will have to set up your phone on a tripod, and then use the self-timer, preferably at the 10-second setting, and then you can tap the shutter, and quickly get into position and the camera will take a flawless shot for you. This ultra-wide lens captures great details with a high dynamic range, which gives you more flexibility to edit your photos and still retain the quality. It is quite amazing how much you can do with just your iPhone camera and a tripod.

The last lens is the wide-angle lens, which is what your camera uses by default. This is good for taking a portrait image, or a groupie, as it covers a wider space than the telephoto lens, but not as much as the ultra-wide.

The best part about iPhone 12 Pro is that all of the cameras are 12MP, which means you do not have to compromise quality with any of the lenses.

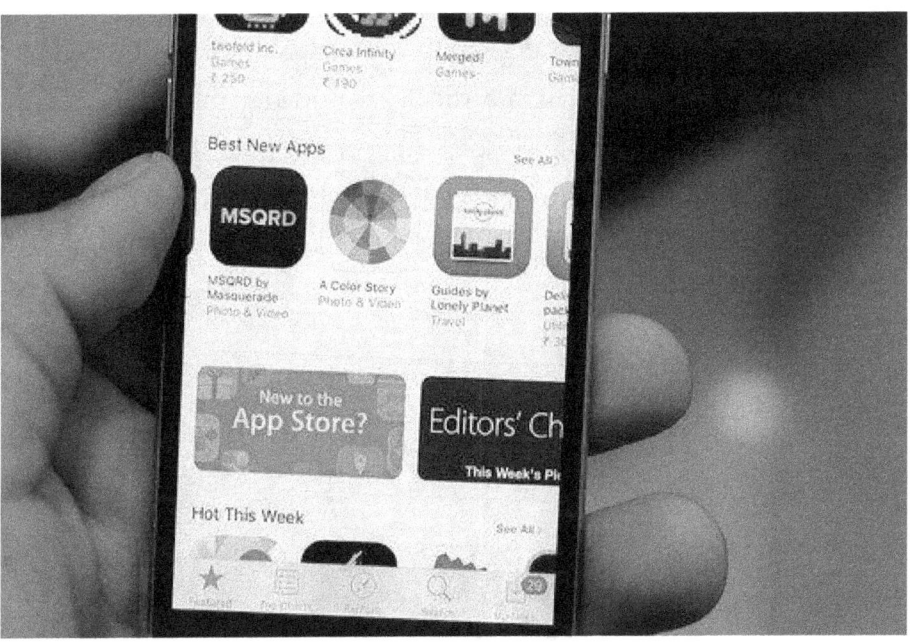

Figure 58: Accessing iPhone Apps

With both the front camera and the back camera, you can select the portrait mode, which will make the background blurry. Using the portrait mode, your photos could look like it was taken by a DSLR.

The blur around the subject can sometimes blend into the person as well, but it is usually not very significant, so much so that a little careful focusing can help with the issue. This portrait mode is a relatively new technology in the smartphone world, even though many photography experts have been using it to create great photos with a professional and aesthetic look.

Selfie Cameras

The selfie camera of the iPhone 12 Pro has some updates as well. It now comes with night and deep fusion mode, that enables your selfies to capture more details when shooting a scene. You also get other features like portrait mode for in-depth selfies. The selfie camera night mode and deep fusion are able to make your selfies look more detailed than ever before, but it's not a world of difference.

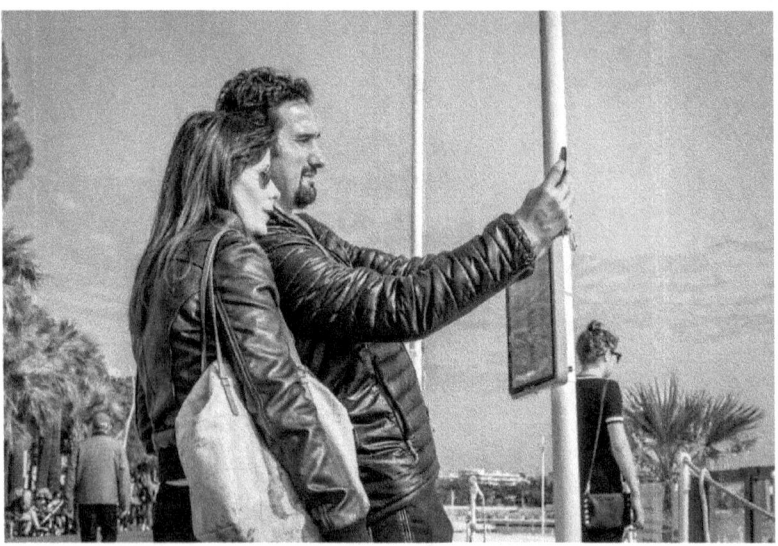

Figure 59: Never a Dull Moment with the Selfie

Taking a Selfie

- To take a selfie, you can use the front-facing camera in Photo mode
- Tap the perspective flip button to activate the front-facing camera
- Hold the phone such that it is in front of you
- Tap the arrows inside the frame to increase the field of view to capture more objects within the frame
- Tap the shutter button to capture the shot. You can equally use the volume button in capturing the shot

Taking a Slofie

The TrueDepth camera on the iPhone 12 Pro front-facing camera allows it to be able to capture 120 fps slo-mo videos, which opens up a new feature that Apple refers to as "Slofies." Slofies are slow-motion similar to the slo-mo videos available from the rear-facing camera in prior iPhones only that on the iPhone 12 Pro comes from the front-facing cameras.

To take a slofie, you can use the front-facing camera in Photo mode;

- Tap the perspective flip button to activate the front-facing camera
- Hold the phone so that it is in your front
- Tap the arrows inside the frame to increase the field of view to capture more objects within the frame
- Swipe the visible dial wheel to the right until you reach the slo-mo feature

- Press the shutter to take the slofie

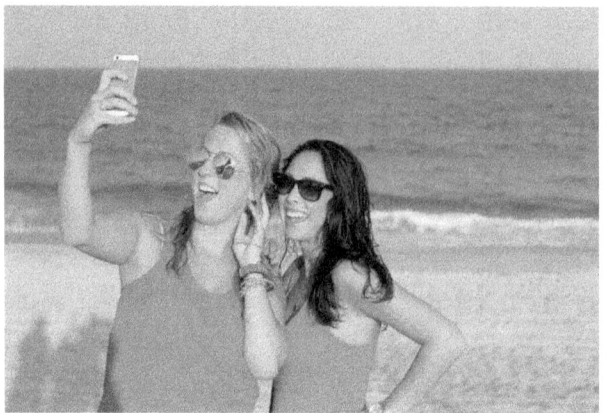

Figure 60: Capture Great Moments with iPhone Slofie

- Tap the perspective flip button to activate the front-facing camera
- Hold the phone so that it is in your front
- Tap the arrows inside the frame to increase the field of view to capture more objects within the frame
- Swipe the visible dial wheel to the right until you reach the slo-mo feature
- Press the shutter to take the slofie

Switching Between Close and Wide-Angle Selfies

- Tap the Camera app to Open it
- Tap the perspective flip button on the screen to toggle between the front-facing and rear camera
- To manually switch between close and wide-angle selfies, tap the arrow button

- To automatically switch between close and wide-angle selfies, you can rotate the iPhone to one side of the phone

Utilizing the Night Mode

Smartphones typically suffer when trying to take pictures in poorly lit circumstances, which is why computational photography comes to the rescue.

Google came up with its own solution and named it Google's Night Sight, similar to what Apple has called Night Mode on its 2019 release of iPhones, including the iPhone 12 Pro. Apple's own low-light photo shooting mode solution combines a mix of hardware and software in getting the phone's photos to be significantly enhanced in dark conditions.

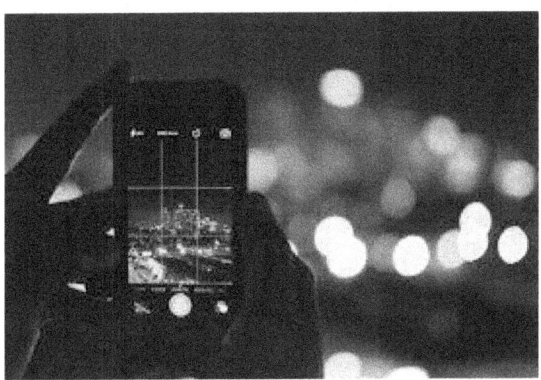

Figure 61: Night Mode Photoshoot

Apple makes use of computational machine learning in Night Mode by taking multiple shots with different formats, which are then fused intelligently to create visible images irrespective of how dark it is.

The night mode is extremely useful in capturing images in conditions considered to be low lights to produce images with incredible detail and color. Apple has designed the use of its night mode to be triggered on its own as soon as the iPhone determines that the available light is not sufficient. Once on Night Mode, a yellow half-moon icon will show up next to the arrow button to indicate that the Night Mode is active. Night Mode will allow you to take photos in low lighting without you needing to make use of flash.

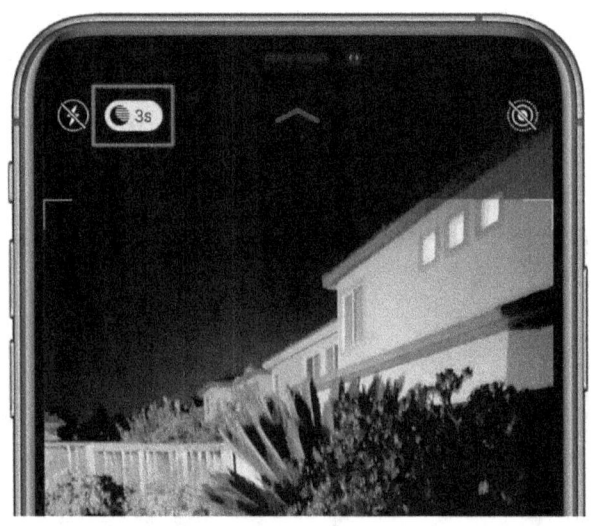

Figure 62: Night Mode Feature Activated

The yellow icon displays the number of seconds (like 1 second, 3 seconds) it will take for the camera to capture the scene from start to finish. The number of seconds displayed is used to determine how long the shutter button has to be pressed down to capture the night shot. This time also can be adjusted. Set too high, and you run the risk of your photo suffering from overexposure, whereas setting it too low will result in a dark photo.

You do have an option to disable the Night mode also by tapping on the Night Mode icon sliding the slider next to the shutter button. For scenes not brightly lit, the Night mode option then becomes available even though it is not yet enabled. You can tell it is not activated if the yellow icon is not highlighted. In such situations, you have to manually tap it to enable it if you think the photo will benefit from the Night mode feature, once switched on, the white Night mode icon turns to yellow.

Night mode adds more details to the final image after brightening the shots in such poor illuminated situations

The Night Mode requires some form of light from a lamp, bulb, or street light to be in the scene where the photo is going to be taken. The exposure time can be set to Auto or adjusted with the slider at the bottom. To increase or decrease the exposure time, simply drag the slider accordingly.

When the shutter button is pressed to take a shot, the yellow slider starts counting down the timer to the end of the exposure, you only have to ensure you're either shooting with the 1x Wide lens or the 2x Telephoto lens for the Night mode to work since the Night Mode doesn't work with the 0.5x Ultra-Wide lens. The iPhone 12 Pro's Night mode is one of the most important camera settings on the iPhone 12 and iPhone 12 Pro.

- Tap Camera on the phone to launch it up
- The Camera app can automatically identify poorly lit conditions and change it into night mode. You can also manually turn on the night mode by tapping the night mode button

- A slider that displays the auto recommended time would appear under the frame. Use the slider to increase or decrease the exposure time manually

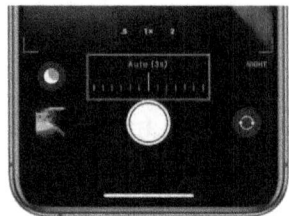

Figure 63: Setting Exposure Duration for Capturing Night Mode Images

- Tap the shutter button to initiate the shooting process
- Hold the camera very still while the timer counts down to zero as it takes a series of pictures that it combines to produce the final output

For best output when you want to take a picture in Night mode with a long exposure time for as long as 30 seconds, you are better off with a tripod. The gyroscope works in such situations by detecting if the phone is still so that it can count down on the long exposure time.

Live Photos and Having Fun with Them

A Live Photo is used to capture what happened just before and what happens just after you take your photo. It is a feature that allows you to shoot a 3-second moving image recording with the surrounding audio.

You can take live photos with your iPhone 12 Pro. It is a super fun feature and honestly, not many people know about it. A live photo is a very short video recording of many still photos, but it can capture the essence of the picture better than a regular picture. It is kind of like the burst shot mode, but even better since you get a short video alongside a photo. You can switch on and off the live photo feature on the right top corner of the screen, whenever you want.

A Live Photo will capture 1.5 seconds before, and 1.5 seconds after the shutter is pressed, it is, therefore, important to ensure the camera stays still a few moments before and after the shutter button is tapped.

It's usually ideal for those situations where a video may be overkill, and a still image isn't sufficient. It is very useful in bringing an image to life with just a few seconds of motion and sound.

Taking a Live Photo

Before shooting a Live Photo, it is important to always ensure the Live Photo icon at the top right of the screen is switched on.

To take advantage of the live photo, follow the steps below.

- Tap the camera app to launch it
- Tap the Live Photos button to turn it off or on
- Tap the Shutter button to take the shot now

Editing a Live Photo

There is also another advantage to live photos, you can tap on edit on any of your live photos and do some fun stuff with it.

Firstly, when you enter your gallery, you see your live photos as a still photo, but if you tap on it, it comes alive. If you tap on edit, you can then take out a specific frame from the live photo and save it to your gallery.

You can also loop the live photo and create a longer video or a GIF with it. There is also another option to bounce the shot, which is a boomerang effect, and it looks cool. There is a third option called "long exposure", which is a picture that combines all the different frames from the live photo and turns it into a long exposure shot.

This is something you can experiment with. You can try out a fun experiment by holding a flashlight in front of the camera and making different shapes with it, in the live photo you'll see just a flashlight moving, but if you select the long exposure option in the edit section, you will see that it looks like you've painted with light! It looks cool. Live photos are incredibly fun, and it has so much you can do with them, so we recommend that you try it out for yourself.

To Edit Live Photos

- Tap the Photos app to open it
- You can identify live photos with the inscription 'Live" somewhere around the corner
- Go ahead to edit the Live Photos

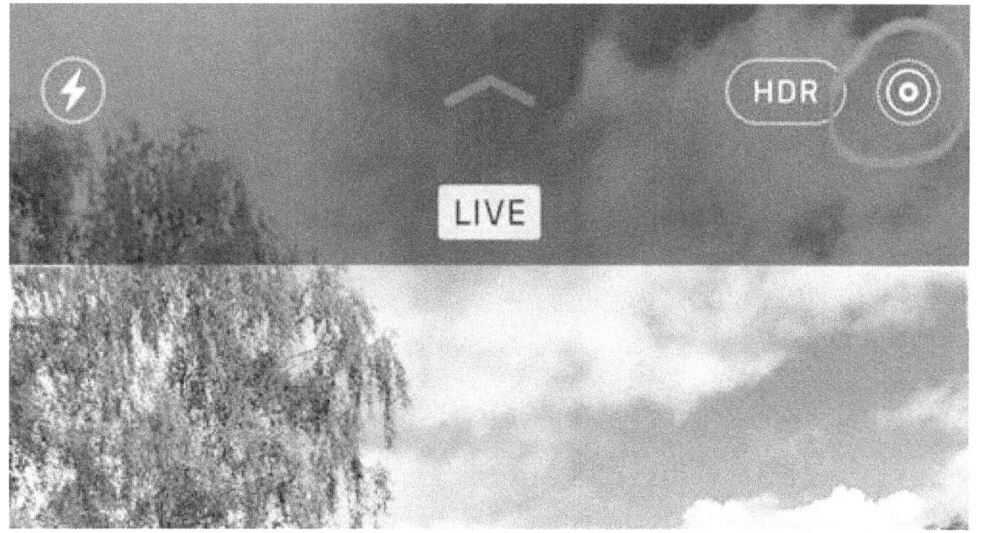

Figure 64: Live Photo Button

Viewing a Live Photo

After taking a live photo, you may want to view the photo to see the result of your action, the best way to achieve that is to view the Live Photo.

To view the Live Photo

- Tap the Photos app to open it
- Tap the image from the gallery of what you want to open
- Hold your finger on the image to play the Live Photo.

Viewing Custom Effects of a Live Photo

To see other effects on the Live Photo, you can swipe up on the opened Live Photo, and four other Effects will be displayed.

You can see all the other hidden ones by scrolling across the effects.

Types of Live Photo Effects

Live

This is the default Live Photo that is used to play a 3-second Life Photo video clip

Loop

Loop will play a continuous Live video loop Photo

Bounce

Bounce will play a Live Photo in the forward direction and then play the reverse direction. This it does continuously

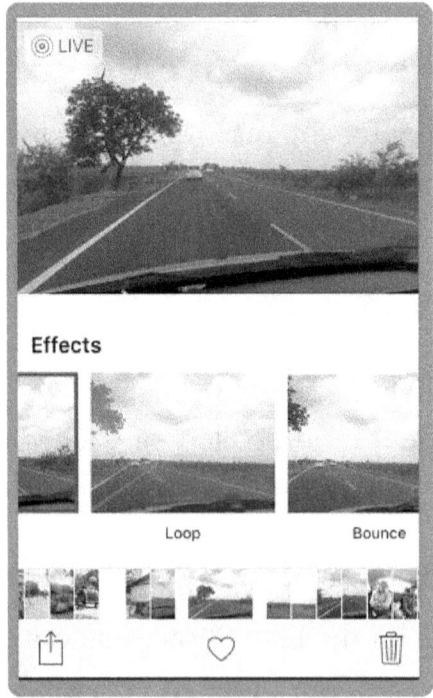

Figure 65: Creating Effects with Live Photo

Long Exposure

This can be used to create a still photo with a slow shutter effect. It is also able to blur any movement in the scene, which makes it a very simple way of creating amazing pictures of a long exposure like rivers or swimming pools.

Taking a Panorama Photo

The Pano mode is useful when capturing landscapes or other shots that cannot easily fit into your camera screen. To use the Pano mode, follow the steps below.

- Tap to open the Camera app
- Select the Pano mode
- Tap the Shutter button
- Pan gradually in the direction of the arrow and ensure it is on the centerline
- Tap the shutter button again to round up the process
- To pan in the other direction, use the arrow
- To pan vertically, you can rotate the iPhone to a landscape orientation
- To pan horizontally, you can rotate the iPhone to a Portrait orientation

Slow Motion Video

The iPhone 12 Pro supports 4k UHD video recording at 60fps or 1080p at 240fps, which means it supports slow-motion video in both the High definition modes. The front camera also has 4k

UHD 60fps video recording, so you can capture slow motion with your front-facing camera as well.

To capture a slow-motion video, you have to open the camera app and slide right to find the slow-motion tab. Within the tab, you can select the frame rate at the top right corner of the screen, you can also change the video quality if you want.

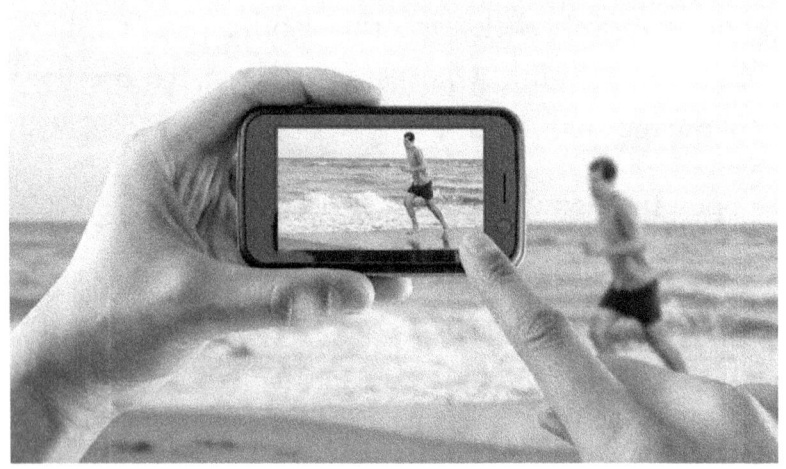

Figure 66: Taking Slo-Mo Videos

Then you just have to simply tap and shoot! After you're done shooting, you can go to the videos and edit the video how you like, you can also take the video on a professional video editing platform and edit it for better results.

Either way, the slow-motion is seamless, with no frame drops, or any unwanted blurriness. You can also select which of the lenses you want to use for the slow-motion video.

Therefore, you can either have it zoomed in, or zoomed out whatever you like. You can slow your video down up to 8 times with the 1080 p/240fps setting. And two times with the 4k

HDR/60fps setting. Either way, the videos look will look stunning, so you are free to play around with them.

Just note that the higher these values, the larger the file size will be, it is important to put these into consideration when selecting your frame rate and the video quality you want to use. Many people find the default settings good enough for their basic needs, only reducing or increasing when they have other specific needs.

Recording a Slow-motion Video

Slo-mo videos record the same way regular videos do, and they exhibit the slo-mo effects when they are played back. The videos can also be edited so that the slo-mo actions can be made to start or stop at any time you want. To take a Slo-Mo video, follow the steps below:

- Open the Camera app
- Select the Slo-mo mode from the options
- Tap the Record button or use the volume button to also start and stop the recording
- You can still snap a still photo while the recording is going on by pressing the shutter button
- You can also set a part of the video to play in slow motion while other parts can play at regular speed by tapping the video thumbnail of the particular video
- Then tap Edit and slide the vertical bars under the frame viewer when defining the section, you want the slow-motion playback to happen

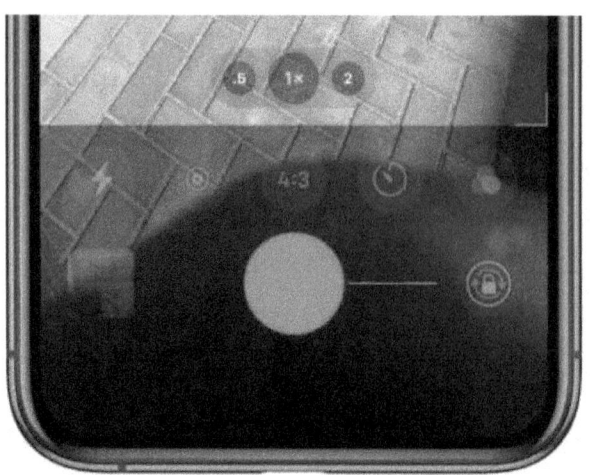

Figure 67: Slo-Mo Capture of Images

Understanding iPhone 12 Pro Camera Focus

The autofocus on the iPhone 12 Pro is already very efficient at capturing crisp and sharp images. The camera instantly detects the subject and focuses on it. However, your goal may not always be to capture the object in front of you, but rather something farther away.

The camera may also struggle to focus on certain objects on its own. This is where the ability to focus while capturing a photo comes in handy. It's fairly simple to focus on your desired subject, all you have to do is to tap on the object that you want to focus on.

Adjusting the Camera Focus

The general rule with taking pictures with the iPhone 12 Pro as well as with other devices is to hold the shutter or tap the subject you want to focus on as you await a white box appearing enclosing the subject. Still holding the screen, you wait for the white square to turn yellow, indicating the camera has locked its focus, after which you can then take the picture.

It can sometimes take a while to be able to focus on the subject finally, but the quality of the pictures will more than compensate for the effort.

Manually Adjusting the Camera Focus

The iPhone 12 Pro can automatically adjust its camera's focus when you are trying to take a picture to produce sharp-focused images. However, there are those who want to exercise more control over what part of the scene they want to be in focus rather than relying on what the camera decides to be the area of focus.

If you want more control over your photos, then you can also try using manual focus. Many people find it a hard thing to learn on a DSLR, fortunately, it is a lot easier on the iPhone 12 Pro

To manually set the focus of your camera on a section of a scene, you simply tap the screen where you want to set your focus, as you wait a white box appears to enclose the subject. Still holding the screen, you wait for the white square to turn yellow, indicating the camera has locked its focus, after which you can then take the picture by tapping the shutter button.

If the photos you want to take with the focus set at the same point are many, you can opt to have the focus locked. To do that, you have to tap and hold the screen on where you want the focus to be set until you see the AE/AF lock showing at the top of the screen, after which you release your finger.

With focus locked, as many photos as you want can then be taken without the need to change the focus point. Whenever you want to deactivate the locked focus, simply tap anywhere on the screen, and the AE/AF will become disabled.

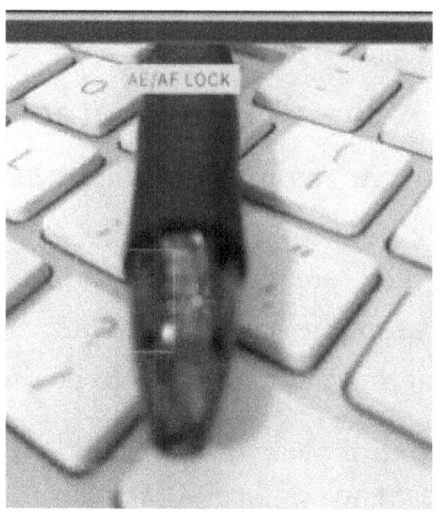

Figure 68: Locking Camera Focus

This feature is quite helpful for taking portrait shots of people and for taking pictures of your pets.

It helps you avoid blurry, unclear, and foggy photos in general

You can play around with the slider to find the right focal length for your subject and then take a photo. This feature is best used with the phone on a tripod or a stand so that the camera movement does not affect the quality of the photo.

Manual focus is important if you want to take crisp and beautiful images of small objects, or if you want to take an incredible portrait or even wildlife photography.

One of the other ways you can use manual focus is to create a 'Bokeh effect'. It is one of those things that we all think is pretty, yet we never learn how to do it.

If you have some string lights, you can hang them up on the background of a person, and try focusing on the person, you will see that the lights behind them become blurry and look like round or hexagonal balls. It is a pretty effect, and you can do this with just a string light, or even street lights.

Manually setting the camera focus allows users to have more control over what parts of an image can appear clear and sharp over the others. When used correctly, this is one simple iPhone camera trick that can turn you into an iPhone photography professional.

Understanding iPhone 12 Camera Exposure

Exposure is one of the most important elements of photography, you don't want your pictures to be either overexposed or underexposed. The iPhone 12 Pro is very good at determining the exposure automatically; it even switches to night mode as soon as it detects darkness.

However, the ability to change the exposure is very useful so that you can accurately determine what kind of brightness you want your photo to have.

Adjusting your brightness levels can improve night mode photos instantly. The right exposure can determine whether or not you actually see the subject. Of course, you can always edit your pictures, but predetermining the brightness really makes it easy and more accurate.

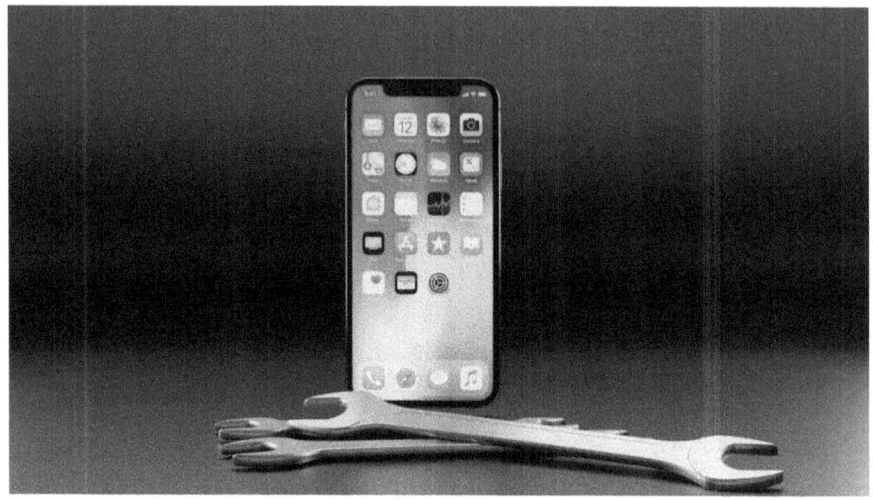

Figure 69: Setting Up Exposure

Understanding exposure will surely help you take better photos. In short and simple terms, exposure is the amount of light that's coming through the camera lens. The higher the exposure, the more light is coming in.

If you're shooting a picture in bright sunlight, it is generally advisable to keep your exposure a bit low, this way your photo does not have a white cast and does not look washed out.

Similarly, with night photography, a higher exposure will mean you are allowing in more light through the lens, which in turn makes sure that your photo isn't dark and invisible.

It's also useful for several different photography techniques, for example, if you want to take pictures of the stars, then you have to have very high exposure, and if you want to take a picture of the sun or a very bright sky, you may want to reduce the exposure quite a bit.

How to Adjust the Camera Exposure

One other fantastic feature the iPhone 12 Pro camera comes with is the ability of the camera to fix photos that appear too dark or too bright. When you have a balanced exposure that does not have any very bright or dark areas that can make the image too bright or too dark, the image can retain its details and color.

To use this feature on the iPhone, you have to attempt to focus on the subject, as explained in the explanation of focusing. When the white square appears on the screen, you will notice a sun icon beside the white line. As soon as the white square changes to a yellow line, you can then move your finger up and down the slider to change the exposure level to what you want by monitoring how bright or dark the image on the screen is in real-time.

However, the easiest way to adjust the exposure is by sliding up the settings and tapping on the exposure icon. You can slide the bar around to see what brightness you prefer and then shoot your picture.

For situations where you want the photo to be a silhouette photo for it to have a dark or completely black appearance, the exposure level will need to be reduced more than normal.

Imagine you want to create an image of a sunset photo, using this simple but powerful slider you take control of the exposure of your photo and significantly improve the quality of your iPhone photography. This is one iPhone 12 Pro feature not many people either know how to use or that it exists at all.

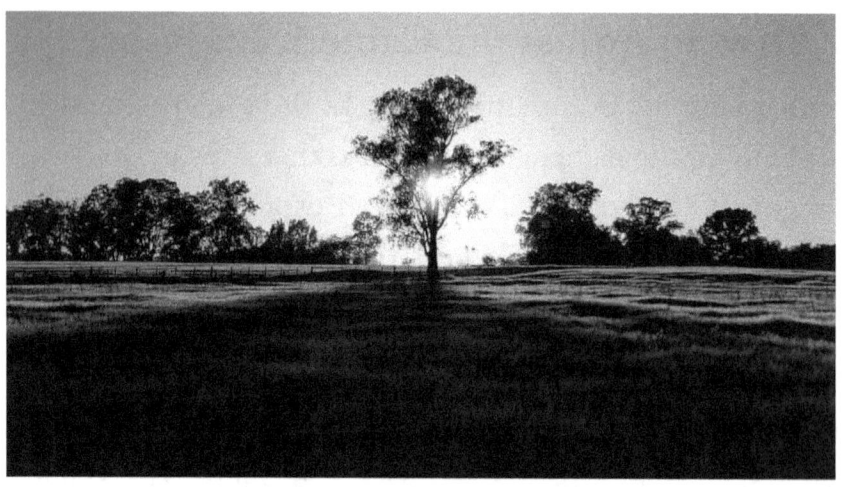

Figure 70: Adjusting Exposure for Effect

How to Lock Camera Focus and Exposure Separately

To be able to separately lock the focus and exposure on the iPhone 12, you have to follow these steps below:

- Tap the Camera app to open it
- Access hidden controls by swiping up or hitting the chevron icon
- Tap the "+/-" button to open up the new ECV control.
- Change the shutter speed and f-stop between -2 to +2 by dragging the horizontal ECV slider
- To get a dark image, drag the horizontal slider to the left towards the -2 mark
- To get a lighter image, drag the horizontal slider to the right towards the +2 mark

- Drag the slider back to zero to reset and deactivate all adjustments made to your ECV.

How to Use the Self-Timer

The iPhone 12 pro allows users to have a 3 second or a 10-second timer on both the front and the back camera. You can slide up the settings from the bottom of the camera screen and slide to the timer setting and set a timer.

A self-timer will make sure that you get in position before the phone takes a photo of you.

The timer is also important if you're using a stand. You want to make sure that the phone does not move or shake when you're taking a photo. So, having a timer will ensure that you're not disturbing it, that way your photos would not become blurry.

Steps to Accessing and Using the Self-timer

Tap the timer icon on the iPhone 12 Pro screen. By tapping it, you can choose either the 3-second or the 10-second timer options

. When you tap on the shutter, the flash will blink every second until the photo is taken. This is a great feature to have if you are a selfie freak.

The timer option works best when used with a suitable tripod stand so that you can set your camera in position without worrying about the camera moving out of focus or out of position when the picture is being taken.

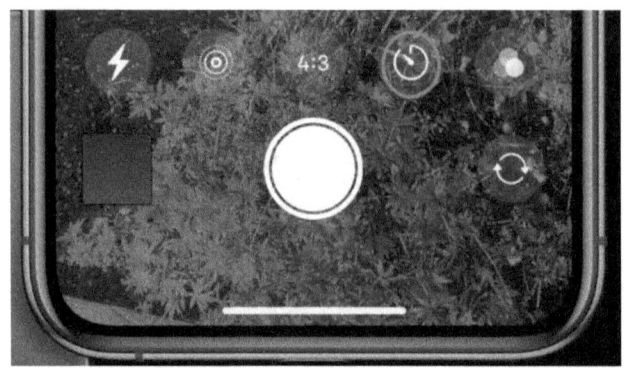

Figure 71: Setting the Camera Self-timer

Having Fun with Your iPhone 12 Pro

The iPhone 12 Pro is not only good at performing various productivity functions but also useful for having fun.

One of the coolest things that you can do with your iPhone 12 Pro is to make a face emoji or what Apple has chosen to call 'Memoji'. It is like 'Snapchat' or 'Bitmoji', but with more advanced features.

The new iPhone 12 Pro allows users to create multiple personalized Memojis that can be used to show their different moods by selecting skin color, hairstyle, facial expressions, earrings, glasses, and other personalized imitations.

This feature is possible by the presence of the iPhone 12 Pro TrueDepth camera's features which makes it possible to analyze over 50 muscle movements of a person's face by detecting and recording the movement in a person's eye and eyebrow, lips, mouth, jaw, cheeks, and chin. These facial features are then transmitted to the Animoji and Memoji characters such that they can express emotions similar to the way you would display those kinds of emotions and expressions. The Animoji and Memojis can then be shared with others in the form of messages and FaceTime apps.

Apple has these Animojis modeled as emoji characters like robots, cat, dog, alien, chicken, dragon, ghost, fox, and many other emoji characters that a user can choose from.

With iPhone 12 Pro's Animoji and Memoji stickers, users can create records of their voices alongside the mirroring of their facial expressions in ways that create stickers that match their personalities and moods effectively.

How to Create your Own Memoji

This feature is available on iMessage chat. Therefore, to access your memoji, you will have to go to iMessage and then set up your emoji.

To create your emoji, you have to tap on the memoji icon at the bottom of the screen, which has a picture of a monkey on it to open the memoji page. There is already an emoji that corresponds to your actions like a mirror; all you have to do is to customize this emoji to look like you.

To get started, it will first ask you to enter your skin color, it has a bunch of different options for skin color, different undertones, and even some crazy colors like green and purple!

After you select your skin color, you can add freckles, or you can move on to the next section. The next section is the hairstyle, in there you have hundreds of hairstyles to choose from, there is something for everyone.

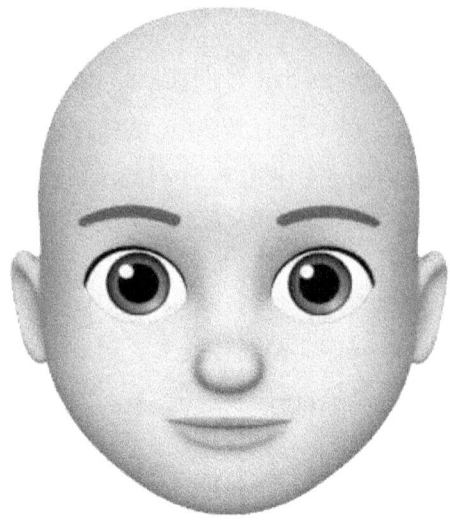

Figure 72: Memoji Face

You also choose your hairstyle, which can be anything from a natural brown, to a funky purple with a green highlight. There are so many combinations possible, it's almost unimaginable. After the hair, we move on to face shape, you first choose your age, which makes it easier for the app to determine your overall head shape, and after that, you can also choose your chin shape.

The next sections are eye shape, eyebrow shape, nose and lip shape, ear shape. You can choose your shape from a library of hundreds of different options. You can choose colors for your eye, eyebrow, and lips as well.

If you happen to have a beard, you can add facial hair as well. If you wear glasses, you can have that too, in any color and frame you want it. There is also the option to add some sort of headgear if you want it, and that pretty much completes your look.

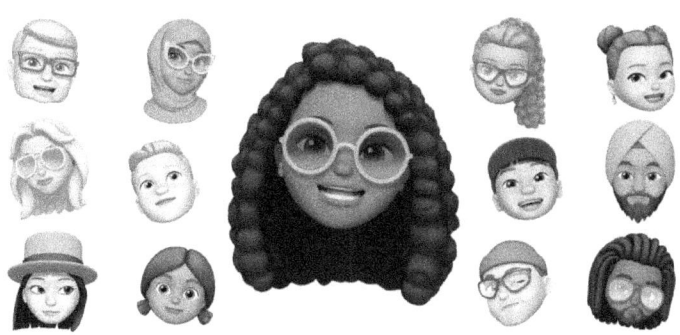

Figure 73: Have Fun with your iPhone 12 Pro

After you've tapped "Done", you're now ready to send a recording of your memoji to your friends doing whatever you're doing. It's a pretty cool feature, and you can have lots of fun with it, by changing up your hairstyle or by changing your headgear, and a lot more, only limited by your imagination.

The fun is not over, you can also share your memoji or animoji using another method that some people consider cooler than the previous method. When you open the iMessage app, you can also send a video directly from the app, and to do that, you have to open the camera icon on the side of the type box.

When you open the camera, there is again the icon for the memoji, when you tap on it, the app automatically adds your memoji face on your real face, so it looks like a cartoon version of you talking to the camera. You can send a photo or video to your friends directly, and you can also save these videos on your camera roll if you want to share it elsewhere.

This process can be broken down into the following steps;

- When in a conversation on iMessage, tap the plus sign
- Tap the Memoji symbol 🐻, swipe right, and tap New Memoji
- Browse through the various Memojis and select the character you like.
- Bring your character to life by adding personalized features that fit your personality to the Memoji.
- When you get satisfied with the outcome, tap Done to add the Memoji to your collection for future use or Cancel to discard your changes

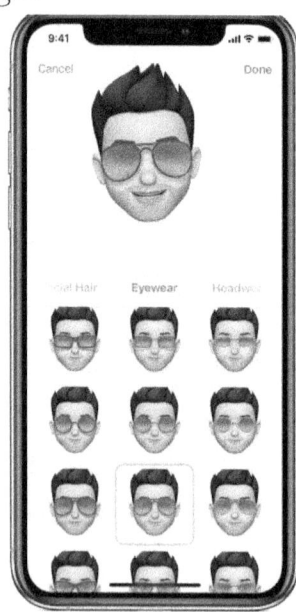

Figure 74: Time to Create Me from my Memoji

To Edit, Duplicate, or Delete a Memoji

If you are no longer interested in retaining a Memoji, you can either make changes to create a more appropriate image of what you want, or you can delete it if the need arises. Follow the steps below to do that.

- Tap the Memoji app and select the three dots at the top right corner
- Select Edit to make the changes or select delete to remove the Memoji from the collections
- Select Done when through or Cancel to discard changes

Sending Animated Animoji or Memoji Recordings

For Animoji and Memoji messages that make use of your voice alongside the mirroring of the expressions on your face, you can create it and send it using the following steps.

- When in a conversation in messenger or tap the button to start a message
- Tap the feature button to select Animoji or Memoji, swipe left, and pick a character
- Tap the record button to start the recording of your voice and facial expression
- To stop recording, tap the red square
- To view your message, select and tap the Replay button
- If satisfied with the outcome, tap the arrow button to send the message or select the delete button to discard the message

Another thing you can do is take a picture or video of yourself as an Animoji or Memoji and add stickers to it before sending, which you can then use in a FaceTime conversation if you prefer to hide your true identity or want to have some fun.

Third-Party Apps for Custom Emojis

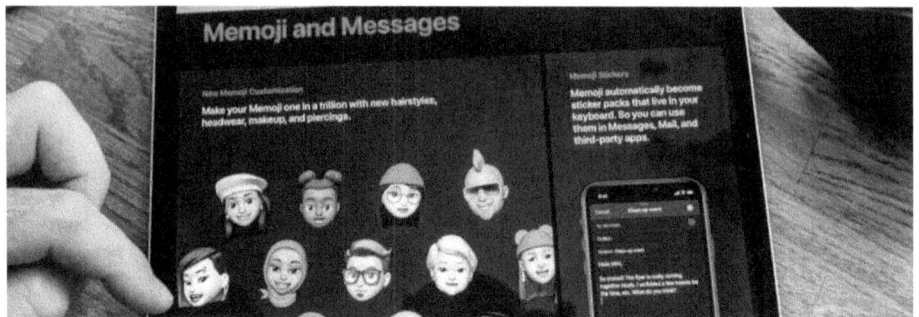

Figure 75: Third-Party Memoji Apps

There are plenty of third-party apps also available on iOS devices that you can use to make your own facemoji. Some of them are a bit better than the others, but you can have fun with any of them.

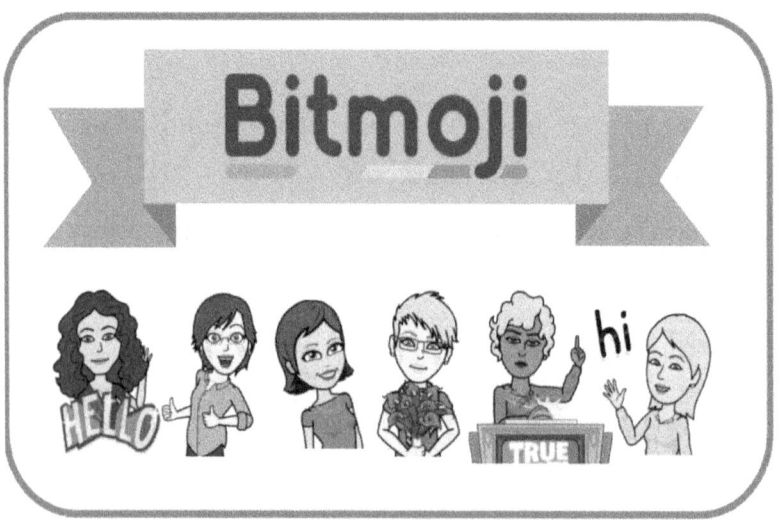

Figure 76: Bitmoji Memoji App

1. The most popular app for a custom emoji is 'Bitmoji'. It is available on the Appstore for free. All you have to do is enter your email address and you're ready to build your own custom emoji. After you have made your emoji, you can integrate it directly into your keyboard and start using it on iMessage, WhatsApp, or Messenger. This app also has a huge selection of clothing and accessories that you can choose from and apply to your bitmoji.
The best part of bitmoji is that it can be used on Snapchat, and that is what made it rise in popularity.
2. Facemoji is another very popular custom emoji app available on the Appstore for free. It is heavily inspired by iPhone's memoji, but it is great, nonetheless. This app also allows you to share your custom emojis on different messaging platforms.

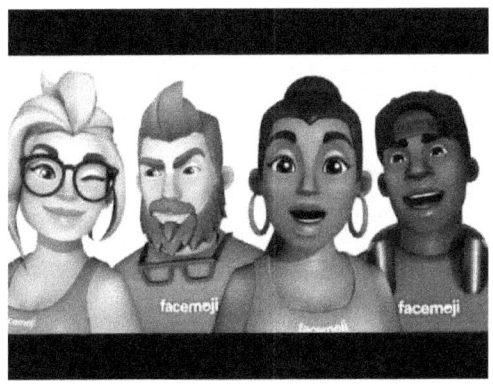

Figure 77: Have Fun with Facemoji

3. Facebook Avatar: Yes, you do need a Facebook account to be able to make and use a Facebook avatar, but it is one of the most accurate custom emojis so far. If you have the Facebook app, you can go to the menu on the top right corner and then scroll down and find the option "Avatar". When you tap on it, they will ask you to build your avatar,

and similar to the other apps, you have to select the face shape, color, and many other options of your choice. You can make your avatar wear a vast variety of clothes too, which makes it possible for you to simulate real life. You get access to a large variety of stickers that you can use on Facebook. Unfortunately, it's not available outside Facebook, but it sure is fun.

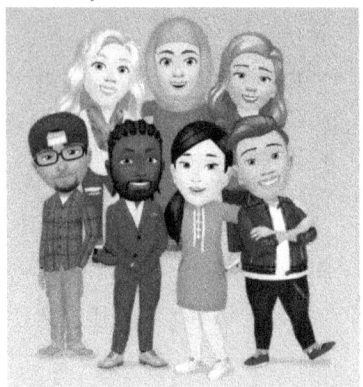 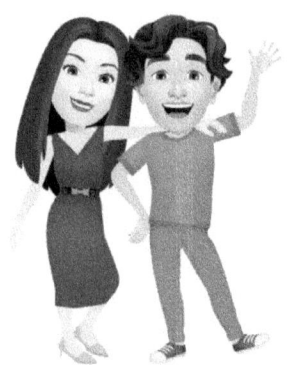

Figure 78: Facebook Avatar

Chapter 6

Configuring Other Camera Settings

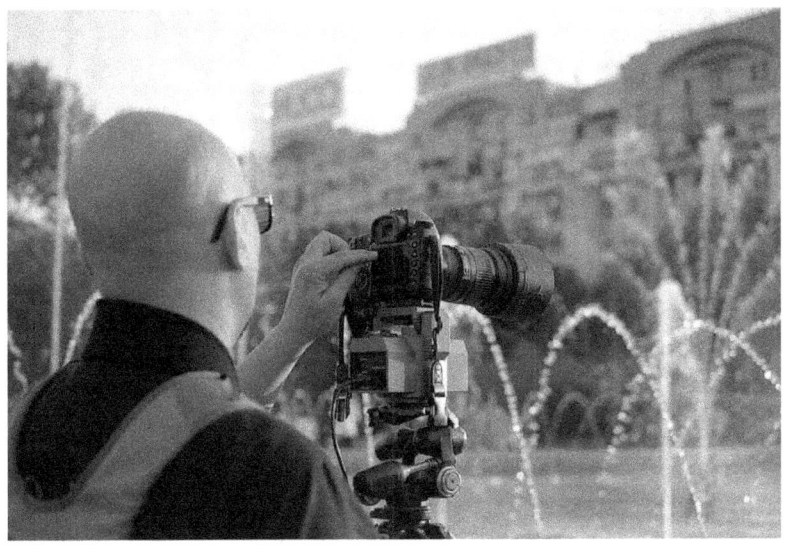

As you may have noticed from what we've covered so far, the iPhone camera seems really simple to manipulate, however, as you will soon find out, there are a few other things that on the surface look easy but do require some level of more in-depth knowledge.

Even though the iPhone 12 Pro comes with standard functions that are easy to navigate, there are several other important camera settings that are usually not immediately obvious except you are able to find your way around the phone.

To access many of these other functions, tap on the arrow at the top of the phone's screen with the iPhone in a vertical position or on the left when the phone is in a horizontal position. This will reveal the various hidden toggles, which can then be hidden again when you tap the button again as soon as you're done. Another way to show the toggles is to swipe across the viewfinder.

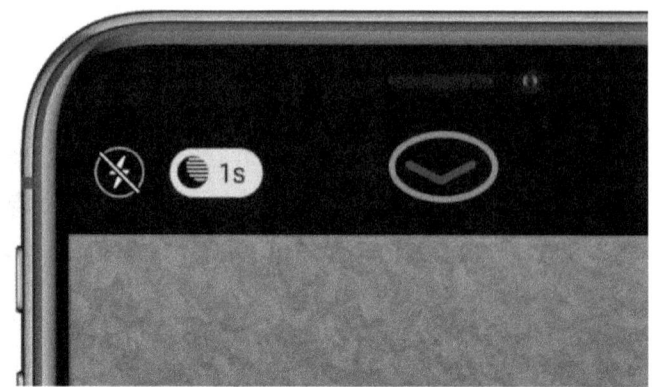

Figure 79: Opening More iPhone 12 Pro Camera Features

Accessing Hidden Camera Controls

Most people don't know a lot of hidden camera controls in their iPhone 12 Pro. We will go over some of the most interesting features in iPhone 12 Pro's camera that you might not know about, and we will also talk about some of the camera techniques that you can use to take beautiful photos.

For a lot of these features, you may need to go to the camera settings and change up a few things. We will talk about the different settings that you may have to change along with the features that we are talking about.

When you tap the up arrow at the top of the iPhone 12 Pro screen or just swipe up on the viewfinder to access more controls, a row of icons just above the shutter button will appear.

Some of the icons you will already be familiar with, others may seem confusing for now.

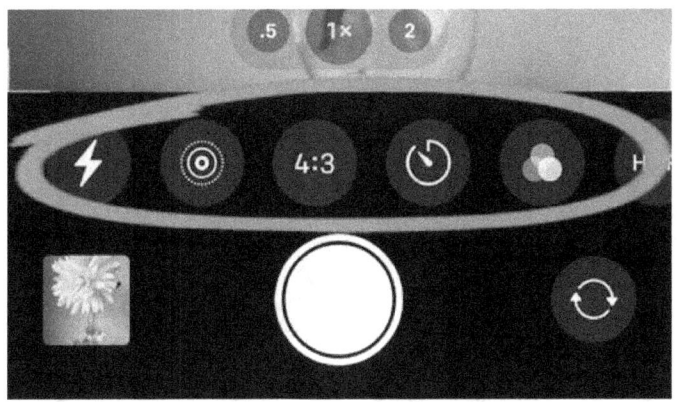

Figure 80: Using Advanced Camera Controls

To describe them from left to right, we have:

- Flash
- Night mode
- Live Photos
- Aspect Ratio
- Timer
- Filters
- HDR

This option provides an alternative to accessing the Night mode, Live Photos, and HDR since we already know that they can easily be accessed from the icons at the top of the screen. It's usually better to keep the Flash setting switched off, except you feel there is a need to add to the illumination of the scene with extra light from the flash. You can, however, tap any of the flash buttons to set it on, off, or put it on auto.

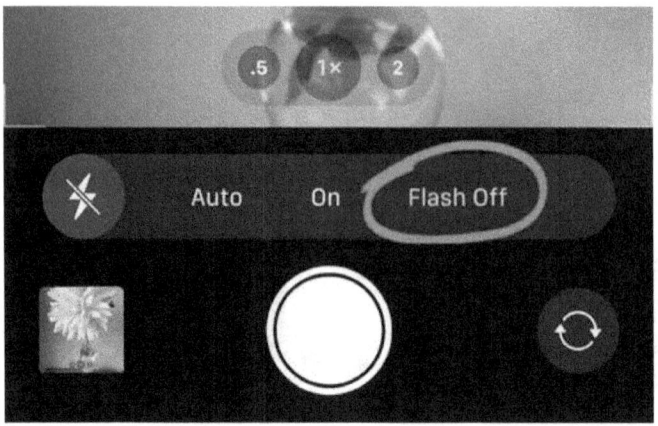

Figure 81: Setting the iPhone 12 Pro Flash

Images on the iPhone 12 Pro can be captured in any one of three aspect ratios that include Square, 4:3 ratio (which uses the standard rectangle), or the 16:9 ratio (which uses the wide specification).

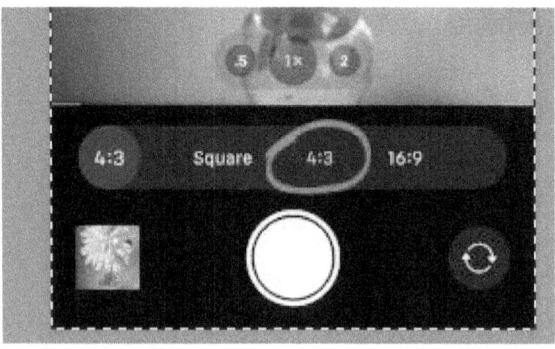

Figure 82: Manipulating Aspect Ratio

The Square and 16:9 ratios tend to always crop out parts of images when a photo is being shot, which is why it is usually better to have photos shot in the full 4:3 aspect ratio. That way, if you feel the need to crop the image to a different aspect ratio, you can easily do that using the iPhone 12 Pro's Photos app or any other photo editing app.

The timer icon can be used to set a delay time of 3 seconds or 10 seconds between when the shutter is pressed, and when the photo is captured.

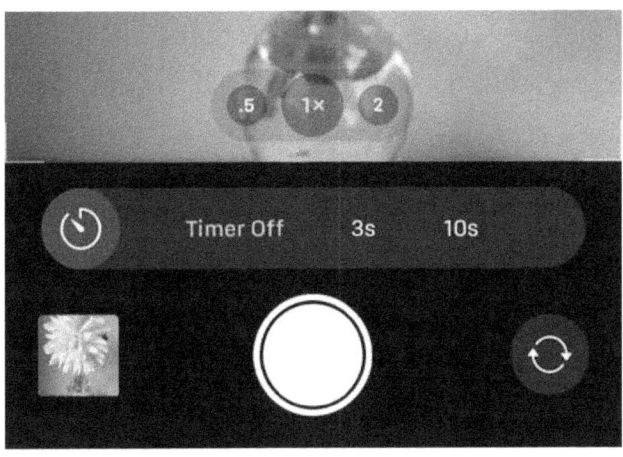

Figure 83: Setting Camera Timer

The iPhone camera timer is handy when you want to shoot a picture of yourself or group shots that you want to be in. A tripod can also be used for the photos to ensure the camera stays steady, especially for photos that require long exposures.

Once you are done using these hidden features, you can decide to hide them again with the controls of the camera at the bottom of the screen. You can then swipe down on the viewfinder or tap the down arrow at the top of the screen.

Using the HDR Feature

A lot of people find shooting scenes with high-contrast to be tricky. Many digital cameras, especially phone cameras, struggle to capture details in areas that are very dark and bright at the same time. But not so with the Smart HDR feature that the iPhone 12

Pro Camera app comes with. HDR enables users to capture incredible details of scenes in both the shadow and the highlights.

Just like the Night Mode feature, the HDR works by taking multiple shots of a scene by using different exposures whenever the shutter is pressed. To create the final output, the advanced iPhone software merges the images to create a single, clear, and crisp image with great color and corresponding details.

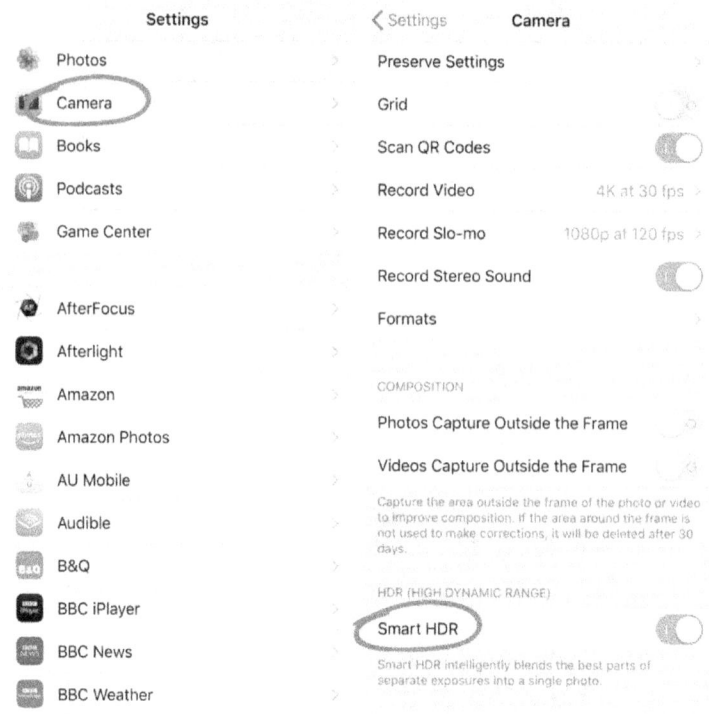

Figure 84: Activating Smart HDR on the iPhone 12 Pro

To take an HDR photo on iPhone 12 Pro, you have to first enable the feature in the iPhone 12 Pro Settings app.

- Open the Settings app
- Select Camera

- Toggle the Smart HDR option towards the bottom of the screen

It is always good practice to keep the Smart HDR on. With the Smart HDR switched on, the iPhone is now able to shoot HDR photos automatically whenever the need arises, so you do not have to bother yourself about whether or not you need to use the HDR when shooting a scene.

However, you still have the option to decide to switch off the Smart HDR if you want to be able to exercise better control over when the Smart HDR kicks in or not. To know if your Smart HDR is switched on, you will see the HDR icon displayed at the top of the Camera app.

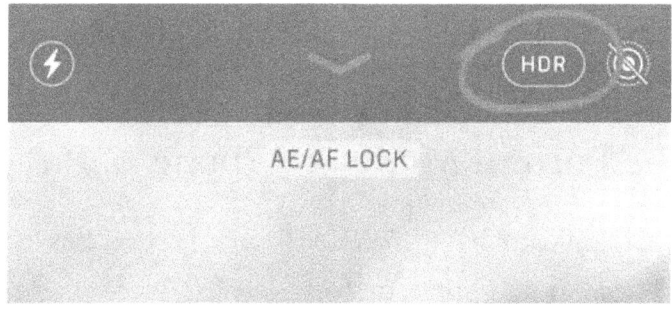

Figure 85: Smart HDR On

The HDR icon can also be used to toggle the HDR On and Off, which can easily be differentiated with a line across the icon, indicating that the HDR is switched off.

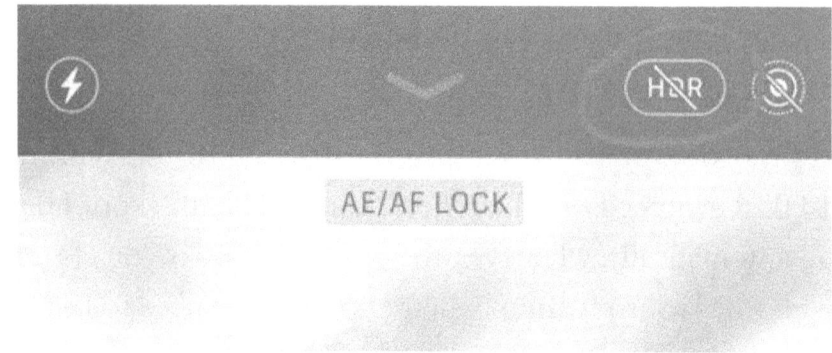

Figure 86: Smart HDR Off

Images shot with the HDR activated on the iPhone 12 Pro tend to have very good color and detail in the shadows as well as the highlights. Without the Smart HDR switched on, some sections of a photo can be too bright compared to if the Smart HDR was on. With the Smart HDR on, many problems associated with exposure encountered when shooting high contrasting scenes can be avoided.

The Portrait Mode on iPhone 12 Pro

The built-in telephoto lens on the iPhone 12 Pro has got great features that make it a great fit for the next level portraits and stills. The telephoto lens of the iPhone 12 Pro offers a field view of a 65 mm lens on a full-frame sensor. This is a preferred range for most professional photographers. The additional zoom is good, but it makes some compromises with image quality when shot on full zoom. The telephoto lens has the digital zoom feature, which gets your photos cropped in from the wide-angle camera.

You can also use portrait mode for shooting photos at night with night mode activated. Just open your camera, swipe right for portrait mode, and follow all on-screen instructions to compose your scene.

Blurring Photos Backgrounds with Portrait Mode

If you have ever wondered how people take pictures of a subject while blurring other aspects of the photos, then you have the portrait mode to thank for that. With portrait mode, your picture can focus on you alone and remove other parts of the pictures that may want to serve as a source of distraction.

To use the Portrait mode in the iPhone 12 Pro Camera app, you tap the portrait mode to the left of the Photo mode below the viewfinder and above the shutter. A frame will be displayed on the screen around the subject whose photo you want to shoot, you have to ensure you are neither too far nor too close to the subject otherwise you will get an on-screen message advising you to adjust your distance from the subject. When on the Portrait mode, you also have the option to switch between the 2x Telephoto or the 1x Wide lens simply by tapping 1x or 2x at the bottom left corner of the screen.

Portrait mode is an amazing feature to use in shooting amazing portraits of people's photos, which helps to keep the person in sharp focus while blurring the background. Interestingly, portrait mode also works well for many other foreground objects, flowers, and pets.

To know that the Portrait mode is active, the words Natural Light appears in yellow on the screen, at that point, you can now tap the shutter button to take your shot.

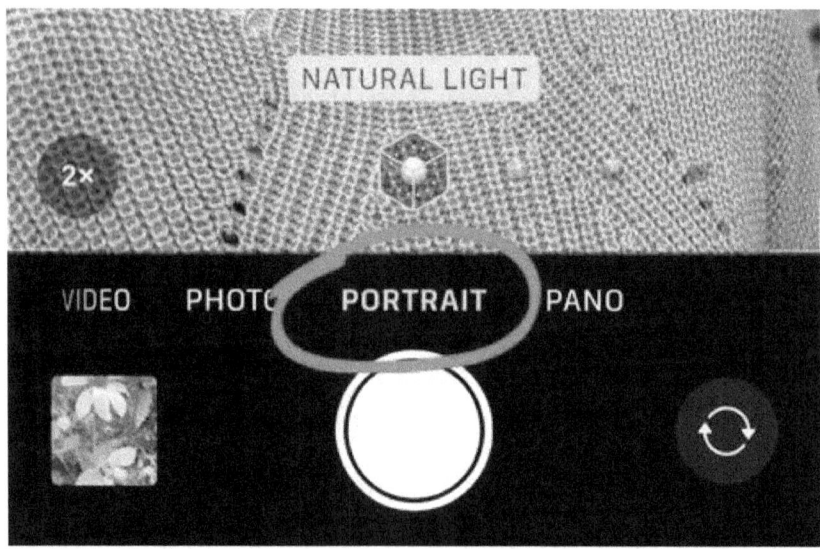

Figure 87: Portrait Mode on iPhone 12 Pro

With the picture taken in portrait mode, you are now able to adjust the strength of the blurring of the background and also use Portrait Lighting to apply some effects like studio light to your image even though many of these settings are better off adjusting after taking the photo.

Adjusting Portrait Photos

To modify your images on the iPhone 12 Pro including Portrait photos, you use the Photos app on the iPhone.

- Tap the image to open it in the Photos app
- Tap Edit.

- Tap the f-number icon at the top left corner of the screen to have the strength of the background blur adjusted

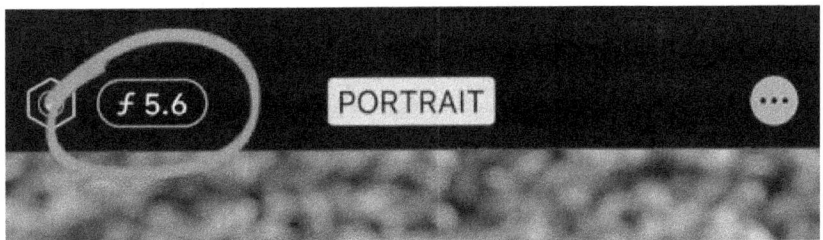

Figure 88: Adjusting the F-Number

To adjust the strength of the background blur, you drag the Depth slider at the lower part of the screen to adjust the f-number. A smaller f-number will make the background of the scene more blurred, whereas a high f-number will make it seem less blurred.

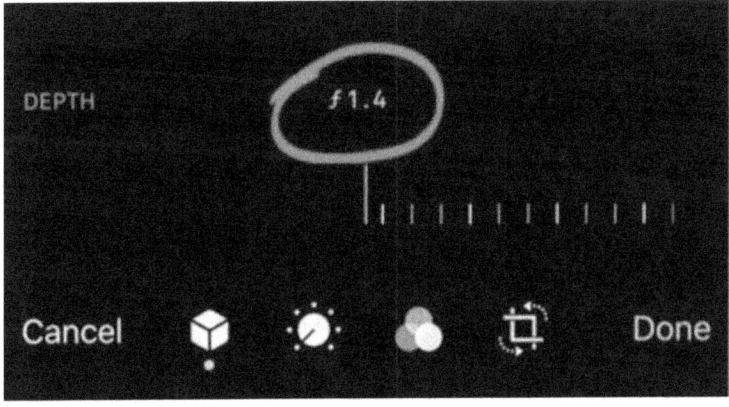

Figure 89: Setting the F-Number

If you want the lighting effect to be adjusted, you'd have to tap the Portrait Lighting icon, which has the shape of a hexagon at the top left and the icons for Portrait Lighting will appear below the photo.

You can then scroll through the different effects to select the one you want from the various options that include, but are not limited to Studio Light, Contour Light, and Stage Light.

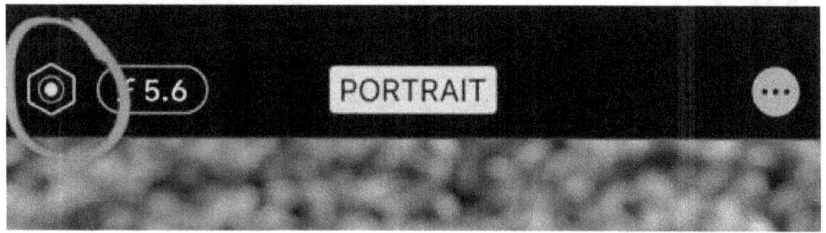

Figure 90: Controlling the Portrait Lighting Icon

Once an option has been selected, the slider below the screen can then be used to adjust how intense the light effect should be.

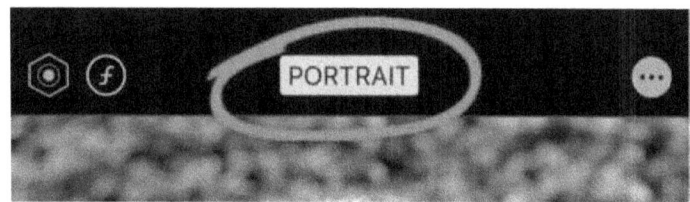

Figure 91: Portrait Mode Active

The best way to see the effect of each of them is to play around with them.

How Not to Include the Blur

If you decide against having the background of your photo blurred, you have the option to remove the blur effect.

To remove the blur;

- Tap Portrait at the top of the screen to deactivate the Portrait mode
- To switch the blur back on, tap Portrait again

- Tap Done to save the changes or Cancel to discard the changes

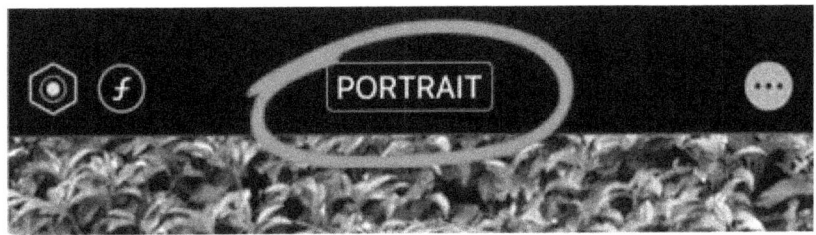

Figure 92: Portrait Mode Inactive

You can then view the output of your Portrait shot as soon as you complete the required adjustments to your Portrait mode photo.

Low-Light Photography

Low light means the absence of brightness or when the scene is dark. When this environment is prevalent, a unique feature comes into play that is popularly and widely known as "Low Light Photography".

Now the question arises; What is Low Light Photography?

In layman's terms, the more light that passes through the lens of a camera, the brighter the picture would be. So, you can determine how much light is allowed to pass through a lens by choosing the lens with a high aperture such as f 2.2, f1.8.

Some basic skills that any photographer is expected to have and know are encompassed in these few tips.

1. Increase ISO: This would mean you are allowing more light to pass through your lens.

2. Slower shutter speed: Less shutter speed is directly proportional to a clearer image as you would get more exposure.
3. Keep your camera still.
4. Shoot images in RAW mode: This is a great feature. Now, not many of us know what that is. This feature allows you to take photos to be as natural as it can be so that you can later edit it. Most experienced photographers take their pictures in this mode.

Figure 93: Low Light Photography

Low-Light Photos with Night Mode On iPhone 12 Pro

Let me tell you the amazing feature available on iPhone 12 Pro. You can take low light photos with night mode available on an iPhone 12 Pro camera. Low light was earlier also associated with iPhones, but it came along with standard iPhone wide lenses only.

The iPhone 12 Pro camera went a notch higher by including this really nice update to be available on selfies, wide, and ultra-wide lens. Whenever you open your camera in a light deficient scene or at night, the low light mode will automatically get activated. When this low light mode is on during night mode, the night mode symbol at the top will turn yellow.

Usually, by default, the camera app will itself decide the length of the capture, however, you can manually adjust the exposure time of the night mode and get more amazing shots. When done properly, the night mode images shot on the iPhone 12 Pro are almost always brilliant and stunning.

Chapter 7

Getting the Most of Your iPhone 12 Pro

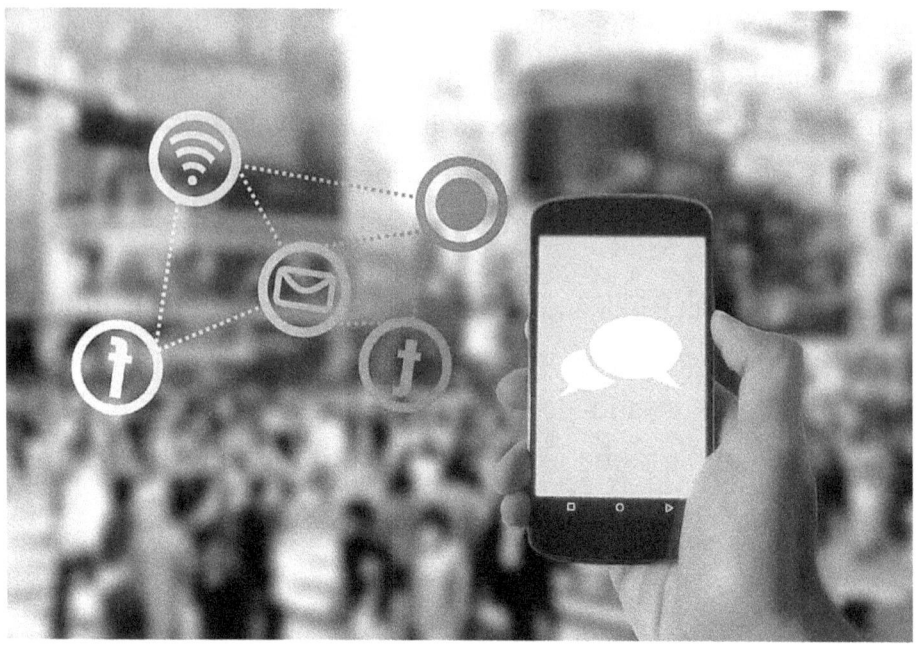

Smartphone photography is a new trend nowadays, and even professional photographers have adopted this trend. Whenever it comes to smartphone photography, iPhones are widely used to serve the purpose. Since this book is all about photography using iPhone 12 Pro, I want to tell you some tips and tricks that are quite helpful in smartphone photography.

The very basic that is worth mentioning is that; you need to have a smartphone that has a quality camera with all proper modes, fortunately, the iPhone 12 Pro has all of that and lots more. These tips and hacks are from the experts who regularly use smartphones for their professional shoots.

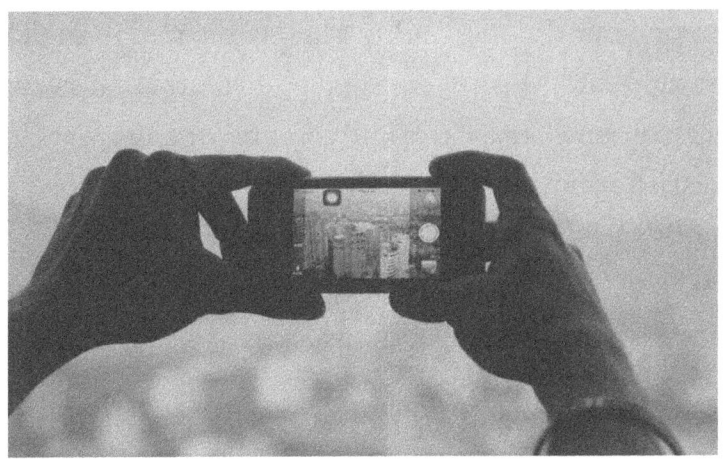

Figure 94: Making the Most of Pictures

Best Practices for Smartphone Photography

Here are a few tips that you can immediately start using in taking great photos with your iPhone 12 Pro smartphone photography.

i. **Always Look for Light**

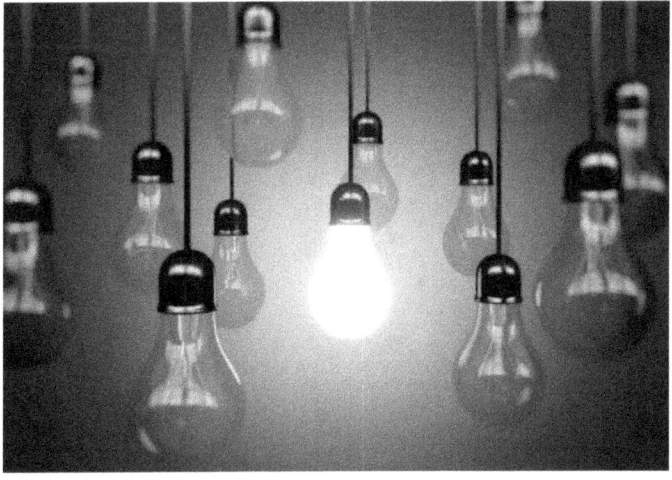

Figure 95: Lights are Super Important

The lenses on your iPhone 12 Pro when compared to the DSLRs are quite bright and sensors are smaller, even then, it is still able to produce stunning images. So, if you are looking for where to get the best shots from your device, then always choose a spot where an object reflects light. If you are capturing shots indoors, then try to keep one window open so that light falls on the person or object whose pictures are about to be taken.

ii. **Focus and Exposure Adjustment**

The iPhone 12 gives you control to be able to adjust 'Focus and Exposure' in a way other phones are not able to so that you can shoot photos or videos to achieve a more desired output. By exposure, it means the amount of light you want in your pictures.

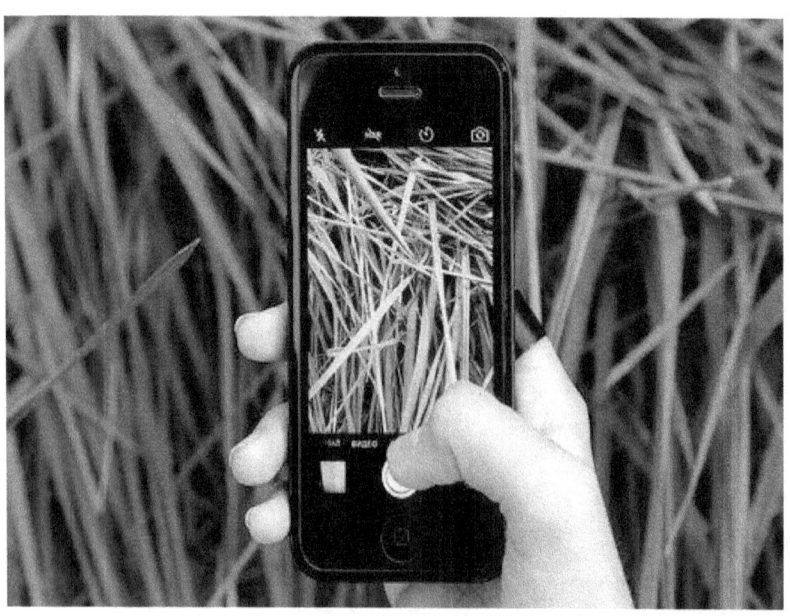

Figure 96: Focusing on Subject

Tapping on the screen is used to initiate the process of activating manual focus. Navigate to settings, you will find a face recognition feature that will help you in fixing blurry group pictures. When you tap on the screen for focus, exposure can also be adjusted at the same time by sliding the dial to either increase or reduce it. You can brighten or darken the image as per your requirements.

iii. **Making Use of HDR Mode**

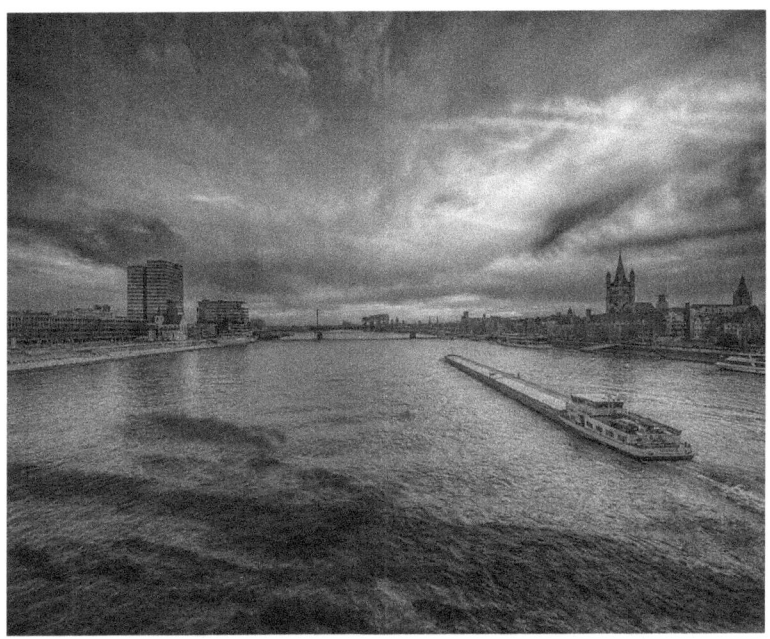

Figure 97: HDR Effects

HDR stands for 'High Dynamic Range'. It is the main feature of many cameras nowadays. HDR is meant to bring the details in your shots, no matter how bright or dark the picture is. It brings an overall color balance to your shots. The best use of HDR can be made while capturing landscapes and portraits. However, it takes a fraction of milliseconds to capture the shot, the wait is worth it. HDR mode gets activated automatically by the camera sensors, you can also turn it on or off manually.

iv. **Turning on Grids**

Grid frames are typically used in SLRs to get better square shots. You can enable grids on your smartphone camera from the settings. This trick is quite effective and helps you in capturing the effective parts of your shots. It is also known as the "Rule of thirds".

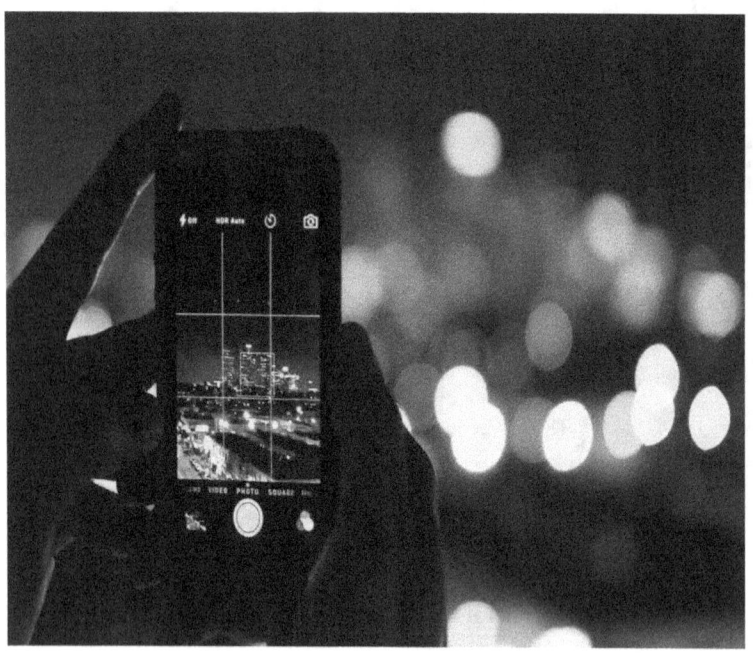

Figure 98: Grid Lines for Frames

v. **Burst Shots**

Burst shots are also a key component in taking great photos that look perfect. If you ever find yourself in a situation where you are unable to capture a good picture for any reason, then you can opt to use the burst shots. This feature captures several images at a go so that you are able to select the most perfect ones among the lot and then discard the ones that do not meet the mark. You can turn on burst mode from the camera settings of your smartphone.

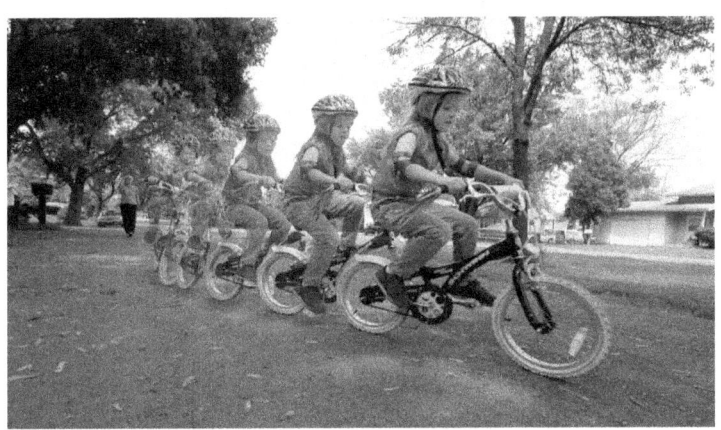

Figure 99: Multiple Images

For most smartphones, you can shoot images in burst shot by long pressing on the shutter button of your camera.

vi. **Try Close Focusing**

Whenever you are shooting a photo where you want lots of the details to show, it is always best to try to focus as close as possible to the subject. This will help you in capturing small details of the subject. If automatic focus doesn't work, you can try manual focusing. Such shots are quite effective in the food photography niche.

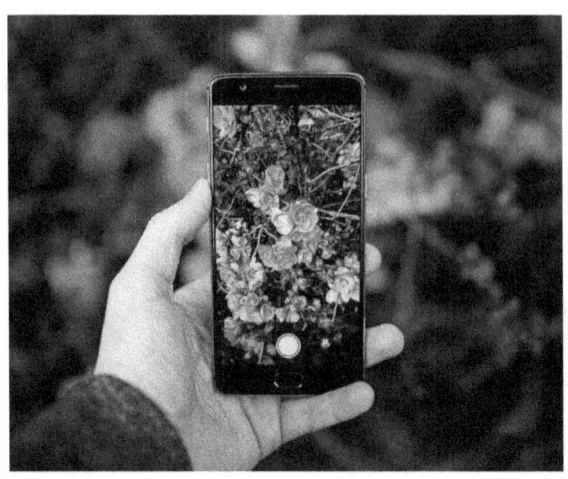

Figure 100: Close Up Images

vii. **Get Used to Your Default Camera App**

There are dozens of third-party camera apps that provide you a lot of features and beauty filters. However, all those applications fail when it comes to clear pictures and basic features such as focus and exposure. You can do a lot with the settings on your default camera app. There are several modes such as portrait, pro-mode, night mode, and HDR. All these features are not listed on major third-party apps. Depending on your smartphone manufacturer, get a perfect guide on your default camera settings from a good book like this one.

viii. **Try Add-On Lens**

Some older smartphones have a single lens that doesn't give good results while capturing shots. You can choose an add-on lens that will help you with a wider view and tighter images. The macro lens adds more versatility to the images and can be used to extend the capabilities of your iPhone.

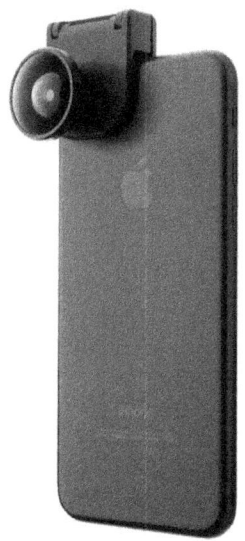

Figure 101: Extending Camera with Micro Lens

ix. **Editing Photos**

Editing photos is what most of the influencers do. You can try editing your photos using some of the best photo editing apps. Photo editing adds effects and colors to your shots, which makes them more effective. Snapseed and Photoshop are some of the popular apps used by professionals.

So, guys, these are general tips for effective smartphone photography which are particularly important when using your iPhone 12 Pro in snapping remarkable photos.

These basic tricks have the potential of improving your ability to take great photos with your phones by over 70%. You can include them to the things you have learned in this book to improve your smartphone photography using your iPhone 12 Pro camera. By now you would know that our smartphone camera quality has a direct impact on the overall quality of images you shoot

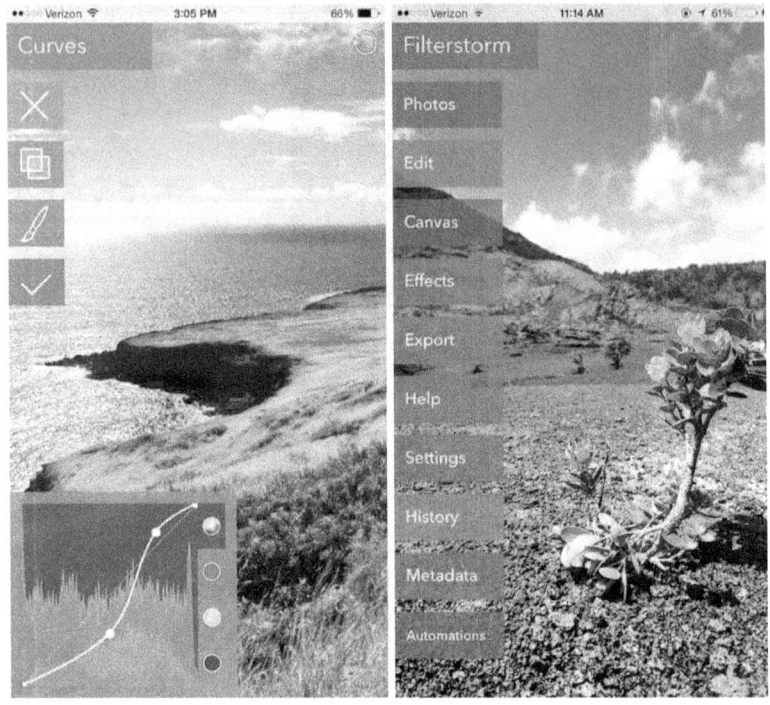

Figure 102: Editing Photos

Chapter 7

iPhone 12 Videography

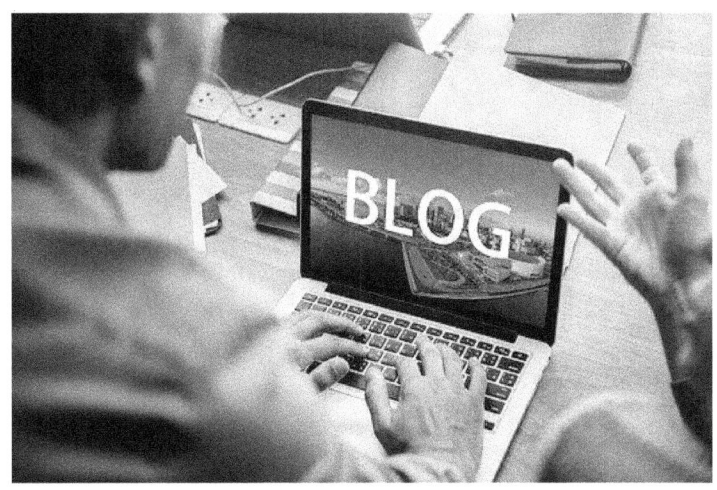

iPhone's videos have always been praised for their high quality and reliability, they rarely turn out to be blurry or unsatisfactory. The video quality is so great, in fact, not too long-ago Selena Gomez shot an entire music video for her song "Lose You to Love Me" on a few iPhone 11 Pro.

The iPhone 12 Pro is even better, it is able to produce crisp, sharp, and vibrant videos, which retain the true colors of the objects and it is comparable to a professional camera.

In fact, with the iPhone 12 Pro, you don't just get high definition videos, but rather, Dolby Vision UHD video at 60 fps. You also get 4K video recording at 60fps. This means that you can shoot professional-quality videos with just this smartphone. Now that we have discussed how great the video quality is, let's talk about how to get the best videos from your device.

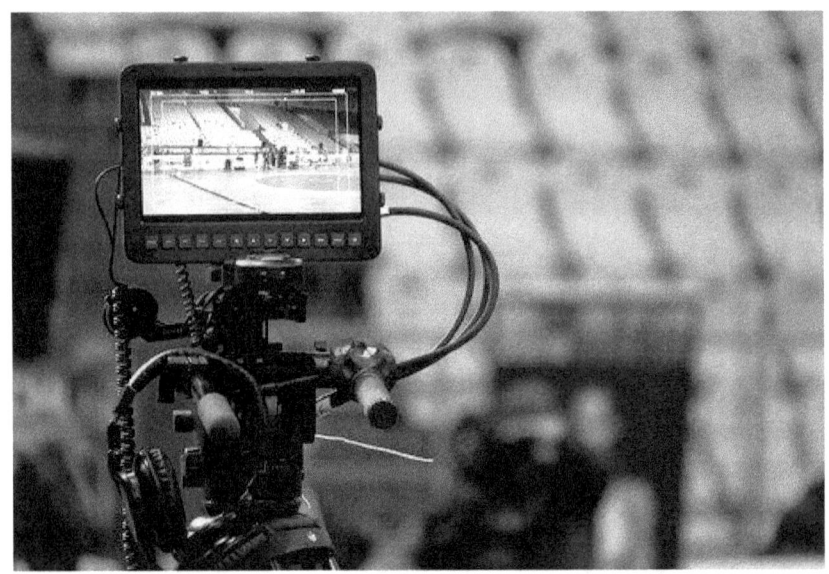

Figure 103: iPhone Videography

Video Quality

The iPhone 12 is the first series of Apple phones to shoot videos in HDR mode. It gives enhanced image quality. The video footage with the help of the HDR mode looks more detailed. However, some flickering happens to videos when shot indoors that have no good lighting. You can record slow-motion video and time-lapse too. The video recording with iPhone 12 Pro has really got the attention of cinema bloggers. Motion aspects also have been optimized very well.

How to Shoot Videos with your iPhone 12 Pro

Generally, you would not be required to shoot your videos at the UHD or 4K setting to get an awesome video. Videos recorded at 4K are quite large and take up a lot of space on your phone. So which setting should you use for your regular day to day videos? You have so many different possibilities.

You can shoot at 1080p at 30 or 60 fps or use a lower setting of 720p with 30 fps, or if you want it to be the slightly better quality you can also use the UHD setting at 30 fps if you want.

If you are just trying to make a birthday video, or a simple video, which you don't intend to edit at all, you should always use the 30fps setting so that the video does not take up a lot of space on your phone. However, if you decide that you want to edit your video and add some cool effects, then you should choose 60 fps as it gives you more flexibility while editing. The video resolution is really up to you. If you make videos for YouTube, then you should use a better resolution, if it's for personal use then it's simply not necessary.

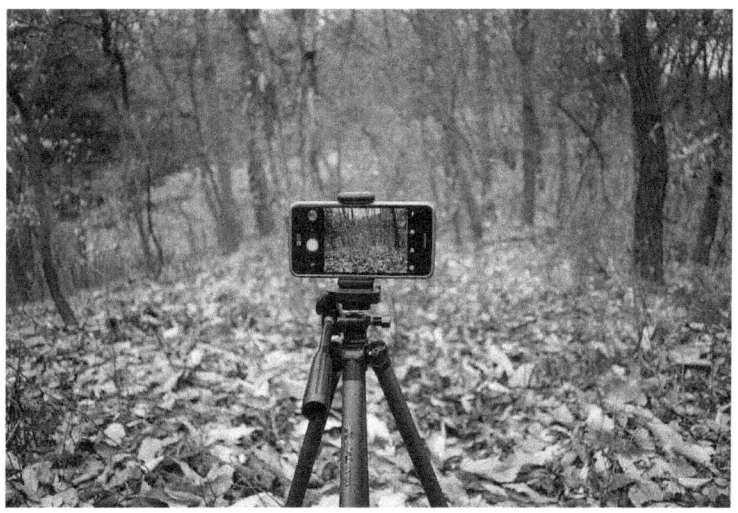

Figure 104: Editing Photos

One of the best things about the iPhone 12 pro camera is the flexibility of being able to choose from a lot of options. Apart from the resolution and the fps, you can also choose different lenses.

As we have already discussed earlier, you can switch between different lenses while taking the video, which gives you the option to zoom in and out of the video quite easily. The change of lenses only gives you about 3X zoom, but you can pinch and zoom on the screen up to 6x. Even at a 6x zoom, the video looks quite nice.

Now that we have gone over some of the general settings you need to consider before recording a video, it is time for us to take a video. Everyone knows how to take a video, you simply tap on the button and it starts recording, but there are more that you should know.

Similar to photography, you can also lock in your focus on a particular object so that the object is always in focus. In the video mode, you have more control over the exposure because you can slide up the options at the bottom of the screen and adjust the exposure to suit your needs. Also, you get to choose the brightness when you tap on the screen for focus.

It is important to understand that exposure is the amount of light that comes in through the camera, while brightness is a factor controlled by the software, so they are separate things, but work very similarly.

Since you can use both the exposure setting and the brightness setting together, you get a lot of control over how bright or dark your video is. If you're taking a video during the night, the night mode activates automatically, and you don't have to do anything to adjust it, however, if you think that the video is too dark, you can adjust the exposure and get a better video.

Time-Lapse Videos

We have already talked about Slow-motion videos, but there is another fun thing that you can do, namely time-lapse. You may have seen movies or TV shows that make use of certain scenes where they show a very fast transition from the night to the daytime, which is a time-lapse.

As the name suggests, a time-lapse video is where you take a video for a long period and compress it down to a few seconds or minutes. It is a bit of a pain to record it, as it takes a long time, but the results are truly satisfying to watch.

There is a time-lapse video section if you swipe to the left. Time-lapse videos are a compilation of several photos that are taken over a long period, this is to ensure that the frame rate does not become insanely high.

If you want to take a time-lapse over a long time, let's say, the whole night. In the camera settings, you can choose the interval at which your camera would take a photo, set the interval a little higher for maybe 1 minute.

The standard frame rate being 30fps, it would mean that it takes 30 minutes to create one second of the video. With some simple calculations you can figure out what kind of interval you want the time-lapse to be, and you can also experiment with it and find out for yourself.

In the iPhone 12 Pro, night mode is automatic, so if you are taking a time-lapse at night, the camera will automatically detect it and ensure that your time-lapse video is not too dark.

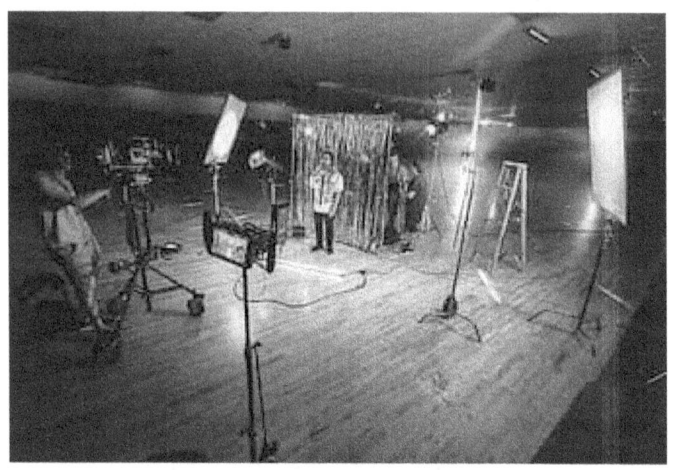

Figure 105: Shooting iPhone Videos

Professional iPhone 12 Pro Videos

If you are an aspiring videographer, the iPhone 12 might be a really good start for you. DSLRs are quite expensive and videography on a DSLR takes quite a bit of knowledge and practice.

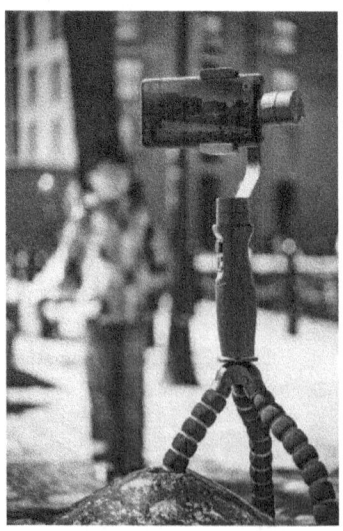

Figure 106: With a Gimbal

With your iPhone, you can get started right away. To get some really professional-quality videos, you should invest in a few accessories. The first accessory that you should get is a gimbal that is meant for smartphones.

Gimbals have a specific function, and that is to stabilize your camera angle and reduce shakiness. With the help of a gimbal, you can also turn your phone in different angles while keeping the footage smooth. Another accessory you can buy for iPhone videography is a simple tripod with a phone bracket, which is a little device that holds your phone on the tripod. A simple tripod will allow you to take incredible time-lapse videos and do other cool photography stuff with your iPhone 12 Pro.

Image Stabilization

Image stabilization in the camera is a feature that is mostly loved by adventure lovers. The ultra-wide lens plays an important role in image stabilization. The ultra-wide camera has got the night mode on the iPhone 12 Pro. Apple has installed a chip that helps in micro-adjustments up to 5000 per second to counter the shakes. Though there may be some distortions expected while shooting the videos, with image stabilization these effects become minimal.

If you compare the image stabilization with GoPro cameras, the iPhone is not out of the competition. You can only see very slight wobbling in scenes while video shooting.

Dolby Vision

Dolby Vision provides you access to a large number of colors with exceptional quality. This feature in iPhones is quite beneficial for the videographers as it captures each color in depth. The iPhone 12 Pro is the first mobile that allows users to shoot, edit, and share the Dolby Vision content. iPhone 12 pro allows you to record videos in Dolby Vision 4k at 60 frames per second. Isn't that amazing?

How to Turn-on Dolby Vision in Video Recording

Well, it is not a difficult task to turn on Dolby Vision on the iPhone 12 Pro. It is easy, follow through with the steps below:

1. Move to the settings app
2. Navigate to *camera and tap on it*
3. Tap on *record video*
4. "Toggle" on HDR mode to enable Dolby Vision

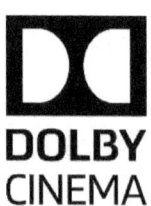

Whenever a video is shot using Dolby Vision, you will see the HDR indicator in the thumbnail of the recorded video. The brightness of the video also gets auto adjusted according to the photo's app.

Drone Photography with the iPhone 12 Pro

If you want to take your videography to the next level and become a top-notch videographer, you can try drone shots. While we are not suggesting that you put your iPhone up on a drone, though it is possible, it is quite risky, as it could potentially damage your phone and your drone, and if it crashes, there is very little guarantee that such a heavy setup will survive.

The iPhone 12 Pro launch video shows us a glimpse of them experimenting with the iPhone on a drone, but unless you are a drone professional, it is not easy to handle it.

Nevertheless, if you still want to try out this cool method, you will first need a very sturdy drone, which can carry the weight of an iPhone, secondly, you will need a smartphone mount, which you can buy online, and then you will have to strap down the iPhone to the drone with Velcro and secure it.

It is not safe to do a lot of things with your iPhone on the drone, but you can hover the drone over an area slowly and fly it at a lower altitude.

However, what you can easily do is, use the iPhone as your display for a far smaller drone camera. Drone footage is often recorded on an SD card and then later replayed on a screen, but if you have the iPhone 12 Pro in your hands, you can get the footage from the drone camera right into your hands.

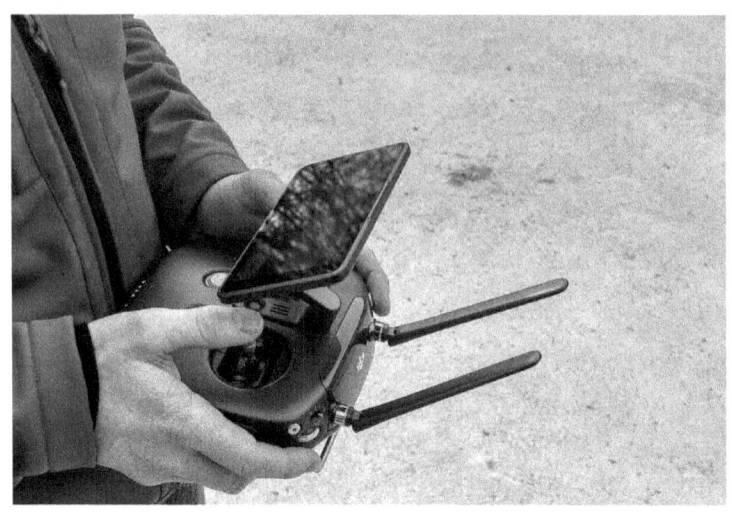

Figure 107: Using your iPhone with a Drone

Depending upon which drone or camera you are using. There are mobile apps on the AppStore, which allows you to connect the camera to your screen through Wi-Fi. Since the camera makes use of Wi-Fi, the range is not very large, but you can still see whatever your drone camera sees in real-time, and you can control your drone exactly how you want based on the video.

Wedding Photographs with the iPhone 12 Pro

As iPhone cameras get better and better, many people are opting to take advantage of its largely superior quality and are opting to just use an iPhone for their wedding photographs. Even some professionals sometimes offer iPhone pictures and videos for weddings.

The iPhone 12 Pro has one of the best cameras so far in the smartphone world, and so it only makes sense that it is going to replace the professional camera to some extent.

The iPhone 12 Pro was launched in October of 2020, right in the middle of the Covid-19 pandemic, when the world was in a crisis, so many people could not hire professionals to take their wedding photos, but iPhone photos are not only relatively easy to take photos in such situations but also very easy to edit and turn into magical pictures.

This is why a lot of people are asking a family member to take their wedding photos, and then getting a professional editor to edit them to perfection. If you want to learn how to take some great wedding photos for your friend or someone in your family, then you must learn some of these techniques.

1. Always search for good lighting. Typically, wedding photographers use a soft light box indoors to illuminate the bride and groom. You may or may not have access to that, so one of the best options is to use daylight. Many professionals try to catch the golden hour, which is between 3 Pm to 5 Pm, depending upon the area and time of year. This is the time when the sun is setting and it gives off a beautiful, soft, yellow light. It is the perfect time to ask the bride and the groom to step outside for a bit and get their photos done. They should face the light source or stand at an angle where the sun is barely hitting their face. Make sure they are not in the shadow.
2. Choose the best angle. The angle is everything in photography. A good angle can mean you use the zoom lens and focus in on their faces, it could also mean you sit down and take a shot where they look super tall. The angle depends on you, and the people you are taking the picture of. There is no formula to it, you have to find out their best angle by working with them and by asking them to pose in

different ways. Keep your focus on making their faces look slimmer, and their bodies looking proportionate. You do not want to make someone look fat, or grumpy on their wedding day.

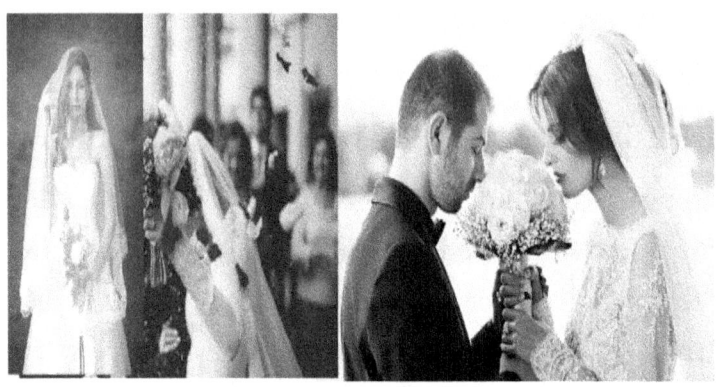

Figure 108: A Wedding Scene with iPhone Videography

3. Keep your focus steady. If you are taking portrait shots of the bride and the groom, then you should make sure that the primary focus is on their face. You can do this by locking the 'focus' on the camera screen to the person's face. If it is a group photo, then you want to make sure that you don't focus on a particular area on the screen, you can let the camera autofocus, and it does a pretty amazing job. You can also take a few experimental shots where the bride and the groom are out of focus, but their wedding rings or their bouquet is in focus. You can take these shots by using manual focus, or by using the portrait mode on the camera app, which can detect different shapes and focus on them.
4. If you are taking video of the ceremony, or just shooting clips for their wedding video, you want to get your gimbal, and always shoot in slow motion. Preferably, always shoot in high resolution, but they cannot be slowed down too much, so choose the highest resolution with the highest

fps possible. The ideal resolution would be 1080p at 240 fps. That said, if you don't plan to slow down the video too much, you can take the video in 4K or Dolby Vision UHD, and then later slow it down during the editing process. If you decide to use high resolution, always keep in mind that the video will look great only on a very high definition screen. Not all screens support Dolby Vision UHD or 4K, so you may be required to compress it later on. However, using higher resolution means you get a lot more flexibility while editing and putting it together. It is generally advisable not to change the resolution for different clips, but you can always compress a higher resolution, but you cannot turn a lower resolution video into an HD video.

5. Have fun with it. You are using a phone to take your wedding photos, why not have some fun with it? You can always try out different filters, even crazy ones with dog ears and flower crowns, and lots more. The best part of a wedding is having fun, so taking the fun into your photos can also be a memorable thing.

6. Learning how to edit. If you take these photos that you took into a computer application, such as Photoshop, or Adobe Lightroom, you can do wonders with these images. You can of course use the phone apps too, but they don't provide as many options as the computer applications do. Your primary focus with editing is to smooth out any blemishes or any imperfections from the Bride and groom's skin and to enhance the colors in a way that takes the photo as close to real-life as possible. There are some great presets that you can use in Lightroom, which will enhance your photos automatically. You can add light beams, and Bokeh effects in the background to make the

bride and groom stand out. Photo editing is a skill you should learn separately, there are plenty of videos on YouTube that you can learn from. It is not very easy, but it will only take you a few days to learn the basics of editing. You need to learn a bit about brightness, contrast, color correction, retouching, and color enhancement.

Now, you're ready to take on a wedding project, so go ahead and create some great pictures.

Chapter 8

Third-party Camera Apps

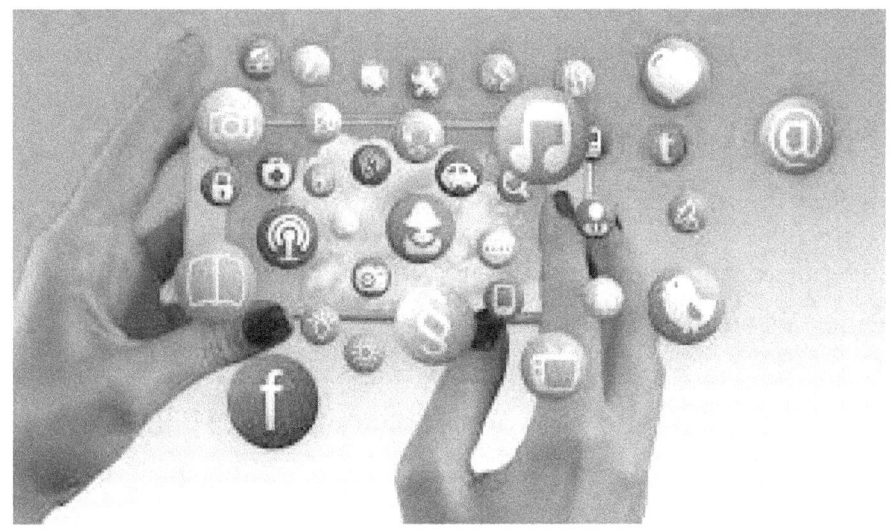

When it comes to photography, the Camera app on the iPhone 12 Pro does such a great job. Capturing images is as easy as the press of a button, however, if you are looking to take advantage of the kind of Cameras on the iPhone, then you may need to consider a few third-party Camera apps.

Camera+ 2

A popular Camera app for the iPhone has to be Camera+2. It has the feel of the native camera app, yet it offers a whole new world of photographic features. It offers extra features like the ability to take Raw shots, gridlines alongside basic functions like continuous flash, 6x digital zoom, and timer. It even has a mode that attempts to detect smiles on persons and a slow shutter when taking long exposures.

Obscura 2

Obscura 2 is best known for its clean and simple interface, unlike other camera apps that bog users down with functions that may be confusing. This app was built to be minimal while helping you to take much better photos. It has a few controls to work with via dials on the screen to control more than 19 inbuilt filters that you can use when taking pictures and even proceed to edit your photographs further and make your work easier.

Many photographers consider it a useful app to have on their iPhone, especially those hoping to leap more professional features. The camera app also has support for RAW captures alongside JPEG, Live Photo, and Apple's default HEIC format. There are even options for depth capture mode, grid overlay, flash control, and manual controls for various tweaks you may want to make

VSCO

This Camera app can also pass as a photo editing app and a very good one at that. With VSCO, you can shoot RAW images and manually control features like exposure, brightness, and lots more. It has a user-friendly interface for both editing and capturing images.

Beyond the simple manual controls, there are many other advanced features, many of which may require a pro-level subscription to unlock. The VSCO also stands out in the area of filters, where you can pick a preset to start editing the images.

Halide

With Halide, you can manually control the photography process. You can use it to set everything from exposure to focus to shutter speed to ISO and lots more.

Although it has an interface that can be intimidating at first glance, it, however, has views for histograms, depth peaking, monitoring of the phone registering, and depth of field settings. If any of these terms sound strange to you, then nothing to worry about as Halide is probably not a feature you want to bother about since it is primarily designed for professional photographers who wish to have better control of the image capturing process rather than having to leave things to automatic settings alone. It is considered by many iPhone users to be one of the best camera apps for iOS devices.

ProCamera

If you shoot a considerable number of videos, then ProCamera should be an app of choice for you. Although very similar to other Camera apps, it provides in-depth control that you can use to manipulate and edit things like the HDR, low light, frame rate, and resolution of your videos.

It doesn't stop there, it also includes some advanced settings for controlling features like geotagging, stabilization, file format, and focusing.

Caring for Your iPhone Camera

iPhone 12 Pro's cameras are already very well protected as they are incredibly scratch-resistant, and also, they can survive a high impact. It is very rare to see that a camera lens shatters. But other things can drastically reduce your camera quality with dust and fingerprints being the most common.

So, what can you do? You should never use water to wipe a glass surface, it only makes the dust stuck on it even worse. There are phone cleaning solutions available, which are used while applying a screen protector, they are primarily alcohol-based, and they are pretty good at cleaning dust off of your camera. It is a good option, but it's not necessary, you can simply use an alcohol wipe to clean your cameras.

Another thing that you can buy is a microfiber cleaning cloth, which is also meant to be for applying screen protectors. They are quite good at catching little dust particles from the glass and wiping them away.

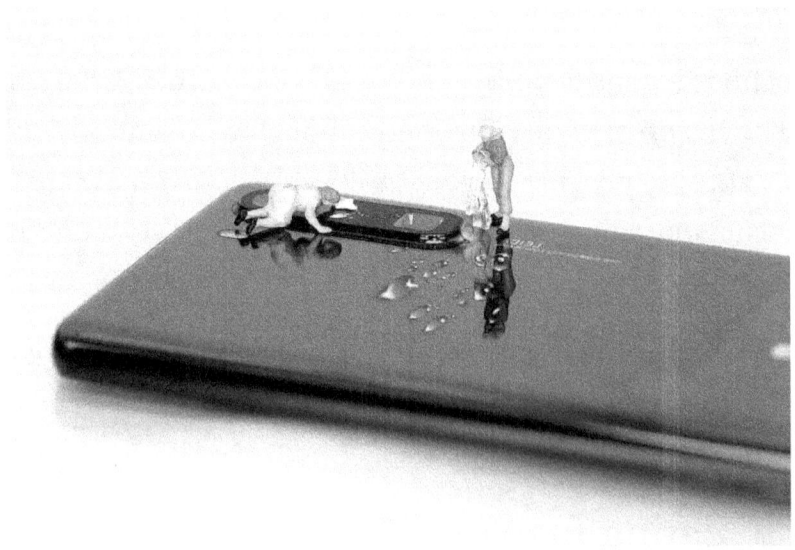

Figure 109: Taking Care of your Camera

One thing that we notice with newer phones is that the camera always protrudes out of the body and creates a camera bump, this happens because the cameras are getting bigger and bigger over time.

To ensure that you don't hit the camera bump in case you drop your phone, you should simply buy a back cover that is thick enough to cover the camera bump. It is a pretty effective way to save your camera.

Conclusion

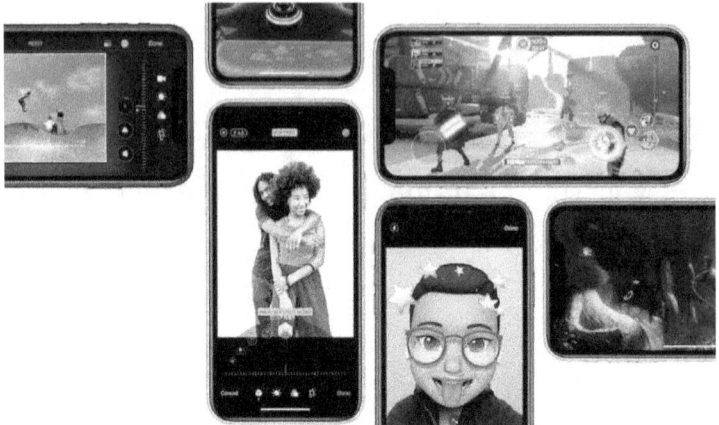

The iPhone 12 Pro has many new photo and video features designed to improve the photo shooting experience of iPhone users and social media fanatics. It has provisions for both beginners, advanced photographers, and videographers. For the first time, Apple responded to the request by users for a Night mode feature optimized for low-light settings.

The automatic setting on the iPhone 12 Pro is now very good at adjusting settings like focus, exposure, shutter speed, and ISO in the capturing of sharp, bright, and crisp images. The portrait mode on the iPhone 12 Pro wide-angle lens can be used to work with pets, and you can easily swap from just taking pictures into making a video very easily using the QuickTake feature in the same way the burst function on previous iPhone used to be done. That means the burst mode is achieved differently from how it used to be.

The iPhone 12 Pro camera has been described as one of the best cameras to have ever been released by Apple and rightly so, and it is not hard to see why. Apple added many features that make the Camera a significant improvement from earlier versions. For starters, the iPhone 12 Pro now has three rear cameras, a standard wide-angle one, a wide-lens one, and a telephoto lens on the physical level and a Night mode at the software level.

This book was written to introduce you to some of those features that this fantastic phone offers and ensure you have a good user experience when using the camera feature of the iPhone 12 Pro.

With the power of the smartphone right in your hand, it is time for you to get excited, and start taking great photos and videos.

With this book, you can immediately get started by exploring the amazing photo feature of this iPhone. Just go ahead and have fun!

SPECIAL BONUS!
Get this additional Book of Taking Better Selfies with the iPhone
100% FREE!

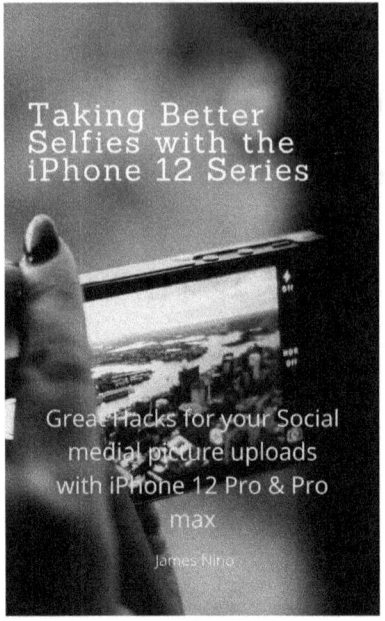

Hundreds of others are already enjoying insider access to all of my current and future books 100% free!

If you want insider access plus this Taking Better Selfies with the iPhone, all you have to do is **scan the code** below with a QR Reader on your smartphone camera or device to claim your offer!

www.ingramcontent.com/pod-product-compliance
Lightning Source LLC
Chambersburg PA
CBHW070639220526
45466CB00001B/228